All You Need...
for Advanced VCE

Business
The Competitive Business Environment

Author and Series Editor:
Jenny Wales

Contents

How competition in the market affects business

What is a market?

What's it all about?

You need to be able to identify the different types of markets in which businesses operate.

Work it out

1 What does Steve want to do?
2 What are the possibilities?
3 What do they all have in common?
4 How are they different?

A MARKET

Markets come in all sorts of shapes and sizes but have one thing in common. They provide a way of putting together people who want to buy something with others who want to sell. Sometimes buyers and sellers meet up but often they don't.

Every business has to decide on the best way to offer its products to its customers. There are often some simple factors that will determine how this will happen.

- Does the customer need to see the product before buying?

- Does the customer need to be on the spot to receive the product?

- Does the supplier need to visit the customer in order to make a sale?

The answers to these questions will help a business to decide on the type of market place that will work best for its products. There is a growing range of possibilities.

Work it out

Decide which forms of market place work for the following products. There may be several for each one.
A haircut, CDs, Christmas cakes, fruit and vegetables, shares in a company, clothes, holidays, watches, makeup.

THE PRODUCT AND THE MARKET

The products we have looked at so far are consumer products and consumer services. Businesses sell them to individual shoppers in the **consumer market**. There are other sorts of market, but they all do the same thing; they bring buyers and sellers together.

Type of market	What's for sale?	Where do the buyers and sellers meet?
Commodities	Commodities include agricultural products and metals. One tonne of titanium, for example, can be compared easily with another.	Commodities can often be traded without being seen, so computer dealing often works well.
Consumer goods	Consumer goods are sold to individuals. They are as different as cakes and CDs.	Consumer goods are sold in all sorts of ways, including in shops, on the TV, through websites, by telephone sales and by mail order.
Capital goods	Capital goods are bought by businesses to help them produce other things. A robot in a car factory is an example.	Mass-produced capital goods will be sold in the same way as consumer goods. Specialist ones are often designed for a particular factory and need a more individual approach.
Services	Services can be provided for both consumers and businesses. Services are provided for consumers by estate agents, dentists and plumbers. Advertising agencies, cleaners and IT consultants provide services to business.	Some services require personal contact. Doctors often need to see a patient to diagnose a problem. Modern communications allow more services to be provided electronically. Accountants, for example, can now work from remote terminals.
Industrial goods	Industrial goods can be: capital goods, such as machinery; goods which are used by industry such as raw materials; services such as finance or marketing. They are important because they are of high value.	Sales and purchases will be made in different ways according to the nature of the product. The examples above show the range of possibilities. Very large deals will often be made between people who work for the companies which are buying and selling.

Work it out

1 Which category do the following businesses fall into: a designer, a supplier of pumps to industry, a jeans manufacturer, a dairy farmer, a manufacturer of specially designed cranes?

2 Where might these sellers meet their buyers?

Sorting out the sectors

What's it all about?

You need to be able to classify industry into the primary, secondary and tertiary industrial sectors.

WHAT SORT OF BUSINESS?

Businesses can be divided into sectors according to what they produce and how they produce it.

The **primary sector** is made up of businesses like mining and farming. They all use natural resources as the main source of production.

The **secondary sector** covers manufacturing businesses. Their products may be used by consumers or other businesses.

The **tertiary sector** includes all businesses which provide a service. These include lawyers, cleaners, accountants, electricians, beauticians, IT consultants and many more.

A CHANGING PATTERN

Across the UK the number of businesses in each sector is changing.

⬆ The tertiary sector is growing because people want to have more things done for them as they grow richer.

Work it out

Sam is trying to work out how to sort out these businesses. Can you help?

1 What are the products of these three businesses?

2 How are the products of the farm different from the factory's or hairdresser's?

3 How are the products of the hairdresser different from the farm's or the factory's?

Draw up a table with three columns. Head the columns with farm, factory and hairdresser. List as many examples as you can of similar businesses. Decide which column to head with primary, secondary and tertiary.

⬇ The secondary sector, or manufacturing, in the UK has shrunk, partly because we buy many products from other countries.

⬇ The number of people who work in the primary sector is slowly declining. Farming, for example, uses a lot more big equipment and therefore needs fewer people. It already accounts for a very small proportion of the population.

What's changed?

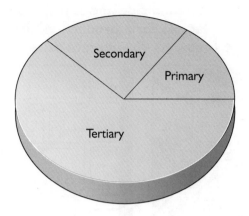

1978

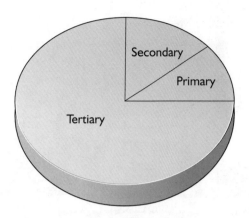

2000

This pattern is found in most developed countries like those of western Europe and North America. In developing countries it is very different. The focus will be on primary industry in the poorest countries. Those which have developed a little more may have moved into manufacturing.

WHAT ABOUT BUSINESS?

Businesses have to look hard at the changes that are taking place in their sector. Being part of a shrinking sector may be good, or bad. If others are leaving, there may be opportunities for an efficient producer to pick up new customers, but more often they will be disappearing.

If the sector is growing, there should be opportunities to expand and develop. Just look at any town and you will be able to see new businesses springing up. Today, these are often in the service sector.

All around the country the pattern is much the same. It is just happening more quickly in more affluent areas.

A MIXED-UP PICTURE

Not all businesses fall neatly into one category or another.

- A computer producer might also run training courses.

- A farmer might also run a bed and breakfast trade.

- A potter might also run a shop to sell the products.

A sharp entrepreneur often expands like this. A business that is building computers, and wants to grow, may find that selling training courses attracts more customers. Purchasers will know that they won't just get the bits out of the box and stand there scratching their heads. There will be help at hand.

Work it out

1. You will have come across a number of businesses in your course. Which sector is each one in?

2. In your local area there may be businesses in all three sectors. Can you identify any? If a sector is missing, explain why.

3. Some businesses are in more than one sector. Can you think of one you know? Why do you think it is in more than one sector?

What makes a price?

What's it all about?

You need to understand how demand-side and supply-side factors for a product, or service, interact to generate price.

Work it out

1 At Christmas there is often a shortage of the toy that everyone wants. What happens to the price that people are prepared to pay to get hold of it?

2 What happens to the price when more is available than people want to buy? Think of some examples.

SETTING THE PRICE

Businesses often set prices from past experience. When asked to explain how it's done, an entrepreneur will come up with all sorts of answers ranging from 'The seat of the pants' to 'We added a bit on to last year's price'. This is probably exactly what happens but, unless the decision makers have a strong sense of the market for the product, it can all go badly wrong.

Price is determined by two factors:

■ the quantity that people want to buy at that price;

■ the quantity that businesses are prepared to sell at that price.

When the price is just right, a business will be able to sell as much as it wants to make – at that price. Customers can buy all they want – at that price. This is known as **market clearing**.

CUTTING THE PRICE

If the price falls:

some people will buy more than they did before

● people will buy who could not afford to before.

RAISING THE PRICE

If the price rises:

some people will buy less than before

● others will stop buying because they can no longer afford the product.

This is all that demand and supply curves show. There is no mystery about them!

IN THE PICTURE

Demand is the amount of a product that customers want to buy at a particular price.

Supply is the amount of a product that businesses want to sell at a particular price.

HOW MUCH AND HOW MANY?

If the price of DVDs is	Customers will want to buy	Sellers will want to supply
£5	250 000	50 000
£10	200 000	100 000
£15	150 000	150 000
£20	100 000	200 000
£25	50 000	250 000

Demand and Supply for DVDs

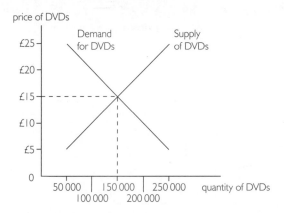

The demand curve shows how much people will want to buy at each price and the supply curve shows how much businesses are prepared to sell. The point where the two curves cross is the **equilibrium price** at which the market clears because everyone has bought and sold the amount they want.

Work it out

1 What is the market clearing price for DVDs?

2 What would happen if the business sets a price of (a) £20 or (b) £10?

3 What might happen if the production of videos stopped so everyone wanted DVDs?

4 What might happen if a new product that replaced DVDs came onto the market?

A McBungle

McDonald's marketing team dreamed up a strategy that they thought would have customers flocking to their restaurants. Two for the price of one was enough to attract any burger eater! It did just that. The problem was that McDonald's couldn't keep the burgers flowing fast enough. Irate customers complained bitterly because they couldn't get their Big Macs. They were offered substitutes – but what they wanted was Big Macs.

Work it out

1 What had happened to the price of a burger?

2 Draw a rough demand and supply diagram showing what had happened. Label the gap which shows the disappointed customers. Explain what the diagram shows.

3 Why do you think it all went wrong?

How much to make?

What's it all about?

You need to understand that supply is affected by costs, technology, physical conditions.

Work it out

1 What might happen to the cost of running Fred's truck?

2 What effect might this have on the price that Fred wants to charge his customers?

3 Draw a diagram showing what has happened to the supply curve when the cost of fuel goes up.

4 What happens if Fred's customers are not prepared to pay a higher price?

PUSHING UP THE COST

All sorts of things can affect the costs of making a product. The spider diagram shows just some of the costs that might change for a pizza restaurant.

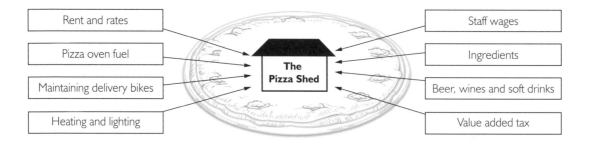

Rent and rates		Staff wages
Pizza oven fuel	**The Pizza Shed**	Ingredients
Maintaining delivery bikes		Beer, wines and soft drinks
Heating and lighting		Value added tax

If any of them rise, the cost of making pizzas will go up. This will have an effect on the supply curve because The Pizza Shed will not be able to supply as many at a particular price.

WHAT HAPPENS TO SALES?

If the The Pizza Shed puts up its prices, customers may go to Fast Pizza or Monopoly Pizza. If they all put their prices up because the cost of mozzarella cheese has risen, people might decide to go to the Chinese instead!

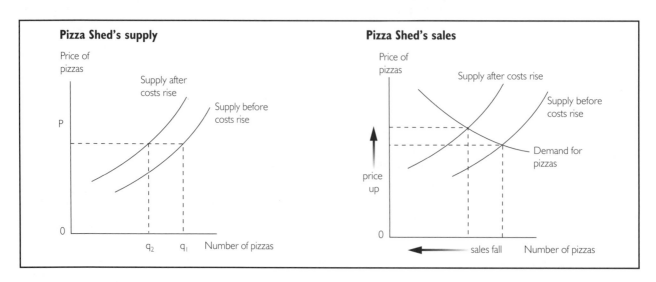

HOW COMPETITION IN THE MARKET AFFECTS BUSINESS

DO YOU HAVE TO BUY?

Because pizzas aren't an essential part of anyone's lifestyle, a rise in price will often persuade customers to eat something else. Many products are like this. There are, however, some lucky businesses which sell things that people have to have. If you commute to work on the train, there is little alternative when the price of a ticket goes up. You just have to grin and bear it.

Work it out

1 Make a list of things that people buy much less of when the price goes up.

2 Make a list of things that people will go on buying even when the price goes up.

3 How do you think this affects a business?

SOMETIMES COSTS FALL

All sorts of things seem to get more and more expensive, but when you look carefully, many products have fallen in price over the years. This is particularly true of electrical products where **technology** has reduced the cost of production. As costs fall, the supply curve shifts to the right.

Work it out

1 Make a list of things that people will buy more of when the price is cut.

2 Make a list of things that people will not buy more of if the price is cut.

3 Create a table like the one below. Complete it with as many businesses as you can.

If the business can put its product on the market at a lower price, it is likely to sell more. Cheaper pizzas can mean more customers. The Chinese restaurant will have to work hard to compete.

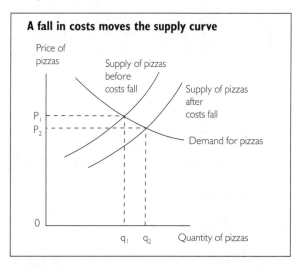

A fall in costs moves the supply curve

Businesses making products that people buy even when the price goes up often suffer if the price comes down. Cheaper rush hour train tickets might persuade a few people to leave their cars at home but there is a limit to the number of extra people who want to travel in the rush hour.

Businesses that make basic foods like sugar and flour also have little to gain from lower prices. The amount we buy is hardly affected by a change in price.

UPS AND DOWNS

Some businesses find predicting revenue very difficult because output is uncertain. Farmers never know what will happen to the weather so they can't be sure how much they will earn. As demand for their products tends to be fairly stable, a surplus will lead to a fall in price and a shortage will push prices up. They are at the mercy of physical conditions.

Business	Product	What happens when the price goes up?	What happens when the price goes down?

Want to find out more?

Taxation and subsidies also affect prices
See **A slice of the cake** page 52
In need of help? page 48

What will they buy?

'Now I really can afford the repayments on the car of my dreams.'

'I'm going on holiday to Ibiza.'

What's it all about?

You need to understand how consumer demand is affected by income, age distribution, tastes, advertising and other products.

Work it out

1 What has just happened to the demand for small cars, and for holidays in Ibiza?

2 Draw a diagram showing this change in demand. Remember – the price hasn't changed.

3 If the average age of the population is rising, what might happen to the demand for this sort of holiday in Ibiza?

4 If the price of petrol rose to £5 per litre, what might happen to the demand for cars?

CUSTOMERS IN CONTROL

Businesses can work very hard to keep their products up-to-date and priced competitively, but they have little control over some aspects of customer choice. This can work both positively and negatively.

More to spend

When people's incomes rise, they have more to spend, so all sorts of businesses are likely to gain. Holidays and cars are two obvious examples. The businesses that sell basic products that we always need are less likely to be winners.

Tempted by advertising

Businesses spend millions on advertising every year. At best, the objective is to persuade people to buy more of the product at the same price. In a static market, maintaining sales may be more realistic. The customers' response is carefully considered by market researchers but cannot always be predicted.

Getting older?

Although Ibiza seems tempting for people of a certain age, others might prefer to take a cruise. In the UK, we have an ageing popula-ion, so businesses that sell products to older people are likely to see their market growing. It might imply that the youth market is in decline, but there may be more than one factor in play at any one time. If young people have increas-ing incomes, the ageing effect will be offset.

Businesses making products that are distinctly age-related may need to develop a broader product-range to meet new market situations. Just making baby buggies or Zimmer frames can be a problem.

What's in fashion

Barbour makes country coats. All of a sudden, their products became the height of fashion. Burbury followed the same pattern. Every super-model was to be seen wearing the famous check. Demand suddenly increased and output was raised to match. This obviously is an appealing scenario for a business, but fashion is ephemeral. Once the trend had passed Barbour was left with excess production capacity and its traditional customers had moved to other suppliers because of the product's new image.

What else to buy?

If you buy a car you must have petrol. If you buy a dishwasher you must have electricity. These products are **complementary** as the price of one affects demand for the other.

If you want a holiday in Ibiza but can't really afford it, you might have to go to Blackpool or Newquay instead. One holiday is a **substitute** for another, and you will be influenced by their relative prices. Many things we buy have substitutes and we choose according to price, amongst other things.

BUSINESS CUSTOMERS

Many businesses make products and services for other businesses. The same rules apply, because all businesses are looking for a good deal. A business which is looking for components or services will be keen to buy at a good price. They will also be interested in efficient delivery. Unreliable suppliers make it hard to get orders out on time.

WHAT'S GOING ON?

All these scenarios can be simply shown using demand curves. The important thing to remember is that people are buying more, or less, **at the same price**, so you must be looking at a new demand curve. It will have moved to the left or right because:

- incomes have changed;
- fashion has changed;
- the population has changed;
- advertising has worked;
- prices of other things have changed.

People buy more at the same price

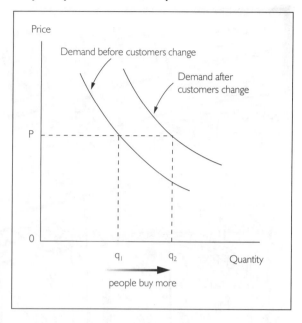

People buy less at the same price

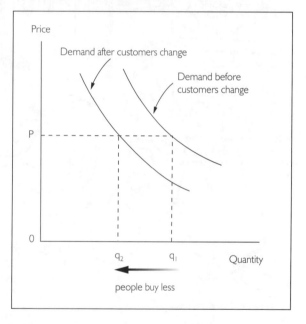

Work it out

What sort of changes might affect the following businesses? Draw a quick diagram to show each change – but don't forget to label them!

A flower shop
A car manufacturer
A magazine producer
A hairdresser
A nursery school.

Is it tough out there?

You need to understand why the amount of competition in markets varies according to different factors, for example, the number of buyers and sellers.

Work it out

1 Why do the shops all have special-offer signs in the window?

2 How might the students choose one of them?

3 Why is it difficult for a burger restaurant to compete if there are lots of others?

4 If one of the restaurants wanted to reduce the amount of competition it faced, what might it do?

HOW COMPETITIVE?

Wherever you go there are adverts. If businesses are prepared to spend money on this scale, it suggests that the world must be a competitive place. Few businesses are insulated from the actions of others. The number of businesses competing to sell a product and the nature of the product will determine just how competitive a market is.

WHY SO MANY? WHY SO FEW?

Some businesses are much easier to set up than others so you find more of them about. The chart shows some reasons why.

Barrier	Type of business	Effect	Business examples
Needs heavy investment to start up	Cars, steel, oil, pharmaceuticals	Businesses merge to protect interests. Entry into industry gets harder as companies get bigger.	Corus VW BP Glaxo Smith Kline
Size matters	As above	As some businesses are only efficient if they are on a large scale, smaller businesses get taken over.	Jaguar taken over by Ford. Glaxo Smith Kline is the product of a merger.
Advertising expenditure high	Detergents, soft drinks, cosmetics, chocolates	Only large businesses can afford prime-time television advertising. Smaller, specialist companies have niches that allow them to compete.	**Big names:** Cadbury's, Unilever, Proctor and Gamble **Small names:** Thornton's chocolates Ecover
Patents	Dyson vacuum cleaner	Because the inventor has protected the product by registering a patent, no one else can produce one like it.	Hoover was fined for copying the Dyson.

EASY ACCESS

Businesses that are easy to set up often have more competition. The service sector is full of small businesses that require little investment. Just look at the number of web designers in your local area, for example. A computer and a little expertise is enough to make a start.

On a slightly larger scale, take-away pizza services are springing up in many locations. You need the facilities to cook the pizzas and some bikes to deliver them so expenditure is not very great.

If you want to start up a small business, these are the types that people aim for. For this very reason, there will be many competitors and it can be hard to make much profit.

FINDING A NICHE

The clever way to start is to think of something new.

- A brand new idea will mean that there are few competitors. The trick is to find something that others can't imitate. You may need to protect your idea legally with a patent, as Dyson did with his inventions, so people can't copy it.

- It might be something that is not yet available in your area. The take-away pizza is a possibility. These are, however, often things that other people can copy, so competition may quickly set up.

Work it out

1 Wherever you live there are businesses. Do they have lots of competitors? Look up some types of businesses in Yellow Pages and make a list of those with many competitors, and those with only a few.

2 Use this information to decide on a type of business that you would consider setting up. Explain why.

3 What effect do you think the amount of competition has on the price that a business can charge for its products?

Want to find out more?

Globalisation
    See **It's a great big market** page 16
The effect on price
    See **How much power?** page 18

It's a great big market

What's it all about?

You need to understand why competition in markets is influenced by the globalisation of economies.

Work it out

1 How does this scenario offer opportunities to UK business?

2 What are the threats?

3 Look at the things in your bag or pockets and think how they offer opportunities and threats to business.

THREATS AND OPPORTUNITIES

The trend towards **globalisation** provides both opportunities and threats to business. In a bigger market, businesses have chances to sell more but also have to face the challenge of more competition.

■ A bigger market can mean more sales. Businesses and customers are looking across the world for inputs, sales and products. People are searching for lower costs, novel ideas and products which have quality or status. Products from developed countries, for example, often have high status in developing countries.

■ Competing with countries where costs are lower is a challenge. If others can make the same product more cheaply, it is hard to justify continued production in the UK.

Newspapers stories often tell us about jobs disappearing because production has moved abroad. Marks and Spencer hit the press when they opted to produce clothing in the Far East instead of the UK.

WHO DO WE TRADE WITH?

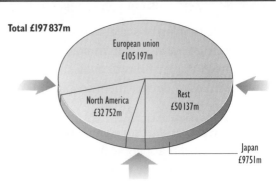

Total £197 837m

European union £105 197m

North America £32 752m

Rest £50 137m

Japan £9751m

Where imports come from

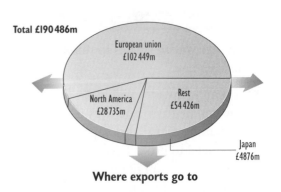

Total £190 486m

European union £102 449m

North America £28 735m

Rest £54 426m

Japan £4876m

Where exports go to

Source: Annual Abstract, ONS 2000.

WHAT DOES IT TAKE?

Understanding a new market takes time and effort. A lack of awareness of local customs and manners can cause problems. In some countries it is polite to refuse twice before accepting an offer of food. Trying to clinch a deal with such customers might prove tricky if you didn't know that. Everyone will starve when the offer of lunch is rejected!

- Language skills are another factor. Although the world seems to speak English, communicating with customers or suppliers in their own language can be beneficial.

- Matching the product to the market may mean making special adaptations for different places. If you make lucky black cats for the UK, you might have to paint them white for countries where black ones are unlucky!

- If countries with lower costs can make a simple product, producing a more sophisticated version can add more value and therefore give a bigger profit margin. Leather goods are made in many countries around the world but the Italians have a reputation for stylish, beautiful products which sell for high prices. Any business producing basic products needs to consider how it might reposition its output for another sector of the market in which profit margins might be higher.

CUSTOMER GAINS

Globalisation means more competition. If businesses are competing internationally, prices will generally be lower and there will probably be more innovation, so customers will benefit. Just watch the speed with which electronic products evolve to get a feel for the rapidity of change in the global market.

THE GLOBAL SCENE

Most governments are in favour of freer trade but it has costs for some economies. The **World Trade Organisation** is the world forum for discussing trade issues. It aims to increase the freedom of trade by reducing taxes, or tariffs, imposed on the movement of goods and services. **Trading blocs** are groups of countries which have special trading arrangements. The European Community, for example, still charges tariffs on imports from outside its borders but these tariffs are steadily falling.

Work it out

1 Watches are produced at a very low cost in the developing world. How do you think producers in the developed world have adapted to compete with these models?

2 Draw a spider diagram to show who is affected by Marks and Spencer's decision to buy products from overseas?

Want to find out more?

The effect of World Trade Organisation and trading blocs on global trade
See **Trading trends** page 80
   Well Protected page 82

How much power?

What's it all about?

You need to understand that the influence a business has over the price and output of its products and services, varies.

PRICE MAKERS OR PRICE TAKERS?

The man who owns the well on the desert island is a **price maker**. He can decide how much to charge as people have no option but to pay up. He is in an even stronger position because everyone has to have water.

A **price taker**, on the other hand, will be competing in a market where there are many buyers and sellers, so there is a great deal of choice. If customers don't like the price or the product, they go elsewhere.

Work it out

1 Why can he charge a high price for water?

2 What would happen if another island resident discovered water?

3 If the two owners of the wells wanted to guarantee their high price, what might they do?

4 If the islanders were fed-up with having to pay such a high price for an essential commodity, what might they do?

The diagram shows the spectrum of competition. Three positions have been marked on it but there are many firms at other points along the line.

Many competitors   The spectrum of competition   Few competitors

Monopolistic competition   Oligopoly   Monopoly

MONOPOLISTIC COMPETITION

Businesses which have many competitors are often selling things that are hard to distinguish from each other. As most people buy on price, there is little profit to be made. They are often striving to find ways to make their products different in order to sell at a premium price. See *Want to find out more?* for further information on ways of competing.

OLIGOPOLY

An oligopoly has few competitors but competition may be furious. Watch the petrol prices in your local area. No one wants to be left behind when prices go up or down. If there is a supermarket selling petrol, you will probably find it leads the market, particularly when prices are falling. In some industries, however, businesses will try not to compete on price as it only leads to reduced profits.

Oligopolies are very common. How many car manufacturers are there? Household and personal hygiene are in the hands of Proctor and Gamble and Unilever. They quite often disguise themselves behind a range of brand names.

MONOPOLY

The solution for an easy life! No competitors! A monopoly has no competitors but is at the mercy of its customers. The business can fix a price but the customers will decide how much to buy. A monopolist has more power when selling something that we all need. A train service is often a monopoly and the quality of the product and the price may reflect it! With no alternative, the customer has to grin and bear it.

Some businesses gain a little bit of monopoly power from their location. If there is only one shop open late in a neighbourhood, the shop keeper can charge high prices. Shops have even been known to raise prices in the evening, when monopoly power kicks in!

Monopolies can be very large-scale businesses and may, therefore, be able to produce things more cheaply. Customers can benefit if prices are low as a result.

Monopolists can have great power, so the government keeps them under control. It set up the Competition Commission to regulate businesses that try to infringe the rules. Look at *Want to find out more?* for links.

THE COMPETITIVE EDGE

Very competitive businesses have to work hard to maintain their position. This often leads to innovation, good quality and service. Monopolists, on the other hand, can be lazy because they do not need to fight to maintain the market. However, things move so quickly now that even a monopolist would be foolish not to keep a close eye on potential competitors. A new invention can wipe out monopoly power.

Work it out

1   Use the list of businesses you put together from Yellow Pages, on page 15. What effect does the number of competitors have on the price a business can charge? Explain why.

2   Do these businesses compete in other ways than price?

Want to find out more?

How to be more competitive?
See **More competitive?** page 22

The Competition Commission
See **Under control?** page 44

At the speed of light?

What's it all about?

You need to understand how changes take place in markets and how market factors may accelerate this pace of change.

WHAT HAPPENS TO THE MARKET?

Markets change in one of two ways.

Businesses change

■ More competition
As some products develop, they become increasingly similar so it becomes harder to make yours stand out from the rest. Microchips are just such a product. Companies are trying to make their chips seem different, but basically they all do the same thing. The businesses are facing monopolistic competition in which it is hard to make much profit.

■ Less competition
When businesses join together, the number of competitors is reduced. Businesses want to do this in order to be more efficient but is also has the effect of reducing competition. If there are fewer competitors in a market, life may be a little easier, although many oligopolists face tough competition. Major supermarkets, for example, are constantly at war to offer the lowest prices or the best service.

Work it out

1 What effect has this change of technology had on business?

2 How has it affected the way businesses compete?

3 Until quite recently BT was the only supplier of telephone communications. What effect did this have on price and the supply of telephones and lines?

4 How do 'phone suppliers compete now?

5 Explain what has happened in terms of the spectrum of competition.

Customers change

When customers change they want different products.

■ They grow richer, so they buy more products. More people can afford things they couldn't buy before.

■ They grow older, so they want to buy different sorts of things.

■ More women work, so they want more labour-saving products and services.

■ Children become more powerful customers, so more products are produced for their market.

All these changes move the demand curve for the product. People will buy more or less at the same price. Have a look at what happens to the diagram.

SPEED

Change affects customers in two ways.

- It changes the products we buy.
  The range of products that are on the market today would be scarcely recognisable to our great grandparents, when compared with things they bought in their youth. Computers, videos and CDs would have startled them all.

- It changes the way we buy products.
  The internet has introduced a new way of buying products and services. EasyJet, for example, has built its business on an electronic market place. In essence, it is little different from mail order. It is just quicker, and cuts out the need for distributing catalogues and other types of promotional material, although many businesses haven't yet reached that point.

Change affects business too.

- Production
  The production process in many industries has been affected by technological change. This process has accelerated in recent years as companies strive to cut costs in order to increase **productivity**. By investing in new machinery, many businesses have reduced the number of people they need to employ, and therefore increased efficiency. Using computers to control stocks has made **just-in-time** production processes more efficient. Supermarkets and car plants, for example, have all been able to reduce costs by using electronic systems.

- Administration
  Offices look very different today. Sometimes it is hard to find a pen because everything is carried out electronically! The savings made by not having to retype things when a mistake is made have reduced administration costs. More and more processes are automated and therefore fewer staff are needed.

Customers change

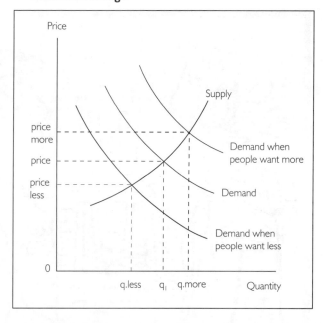

- Marketing
  The output today is subject to constant innovation. Businesses are always searching for strategies to make their products seem unique. The increasing sophistication of electronic techniques allows ideas to move rapidly.

Work it out

1 How has the market for products aimed at children changed in the last ten years?

2 How does the increase in productivity, which results from technological change, affect the supply curve?

3 How has technological change affected a business you know?

Want to find out more?

Becoming more competitive
  See **More competitive?** page 22

Managing competitiveness
  See **Taking power** page 24

More competitive?

What's it all about?

You need to understand how businesses seek to be more competitive by using a range of strategies, such as adding value, improving quality, product differentiation, advertising and pricing policies.

Work it out

1. How might they persuade people to buy it?
2. How can Mandy and Divyang improve the product so more people will want to buy it?
3. How might they persuade people that their product is different from all the other similar ones on the market?
4. What might they do if they wanted to adjust the product in order to persuade people to pay more for it? – Be creative!

BEATING THE COMPETITION

Businesses have to try hard to find ways of improving competitiveness. If a strategy can be devised that makes the product special, customers will continue to buy it even if the price is higher. Here are some of the ways a business might go about doing this.

ADDING VALUE

Adding value simply means putting resources together in such a way that people will pay a higher price for the product and therefore give the business a better return. By turning a pile of bits of wood into a chair, Mandy and Divyang had already added value. They could sell the chair for a higher price than the bits of wood. What ideas did you come up with for adding some more value?

Many products have added-value versions. Most people buy a simple mobile phone but with little more cost, a company can produce a very up-market version carrying a price of several hundred pounds.

IMPROVING QUALITY

Businesses often claim to have 'improved quality' in order to persuade people to buy their product. A better quality product can stand out from its competitors and command a higher price. For many years Marks and Spencer stood out because its products were of high quality. When customers began to doubt this, they went elsewhere.

In a market that is very competitive, a product may achieve an advantage by being better. Many businesses hold awards from the **British Standards Institute** which guarantee quality.

PRODUCT DIFFERENTIATION

By making your product a little different from all the others, you may be able to sell more or command a higher price. Businesses spend a lot of time doing this, if the market is very competitive, because it gives them a little more power. The colour of stripe in the toothpaste or a little horse on a shirt all help to persuade people that your product is different.

ADVERTISING

In a competitive market you have to tell people about your product. Millions are spent every year on advertising. A catchy advert can shift the demand curve for the product because more people are prepared to buy your product at the same price.

Advertising shifts the demand curve

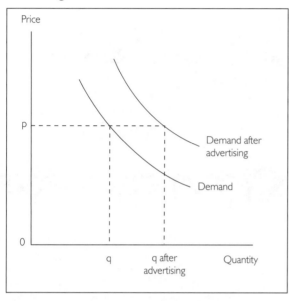

PRICING POLICIES

Setting the right price can make or break a product. People have to think that they are getting value for money. Although price is always decided by the quantity people want and the quantity businesses are prepared to supply at a particular price, businesses can use the strategies in the table below to play the market.

Work it out

1 How have the following products been made competitive? Jaguar car, a CD, a Gap t-shirt, a package holiday, a cup of coffee.

2 Which pricing policy would you use if:
   - ❏ you want to open a shop in an area where there are many competitors?
   - ❏ your shop had been open a while and a new one opened up?
   - ❏ you are one of several shops on the high street?
   - ❏ you are planning to open a trendy café where everyone will want to be seen?

Pricing policies

Type	Strategy	Why?
Demand-based pricing	Prices based on the price of similar products as this shows how much customers are prepared to pay.	Small cars are often priced on this basis because the market is very competitive.
Cost-based pricing	Prices based on costs of production plus a margin for profit.	If overheads are not taken into account properly, a business can end up in trouble.
Price skimming	Prices set above demand-based pricing.	Often used for new products which are ahead of the game. People really want them because they are 'cool' so they will pay a higher price.
Penetration pricing	Prices set below demand-based pricing level.	If a new gym wants to attract members, it often initially reduces its joining fee. This can help it to cover its start-up costs more quickly as it attracts members.
Predatory pricing	Prices set very low in order to push competitors out of the market.	A big business might do this in order to avoid the challenge from new competitors.

Taking power

What's it all about?

You need to understand how businesses seek to manage the competitiveness of the market by using a range of strategies such as mergers, takeovers and product differentiation.

MERGERS AND TAKEOVERS

What's the difference?

Mergers and takeovers occur when firms join together. Mergers are usually amicable as both sides see the advantages. Takeovers can be either amicable or hostile. Sometimes the people who run a business don't really want it to be bought but another company makes an offer that shareholders find hard to refuse.

Work it out

1 Why has the big fish got more power in the pond?
2 If the big fish were a business, why might it be more competitive than smaller businesses?
3 Why does it want to eat the smaller fish?
4 Why do you think some businesses are taken over and others merge?
5 What effect do mergers and takeovers have on the position of a business in the spectrum of competition?
6 What effect does this have on its ability to make a profit?

Why get bigger?

Being a big fish in a little pond is a powerful place to be. Being a big fish in a big pond is not a bad place to be. Being bigger than the competition often means that costs can be lower. If two business which produce one million pairs of trainers a year join together they will be able to make savings on:

- research and development;
- design;
- production;
- marketing;
- administration and HQ services.

These are all known as **economies of scale**.

If the new business can make its products more cheaply than smaller ones, it can either:

■ undercut the rest of the market and make more profit by selling more trainers than before; or

■ stick with the current market price and make a higher margin on fewer sales.

Either way, the business has increased its profit by growing bigger.

Remember the spectrum of competition? If not have a look at page 18. It is very competitive at one end because there are many businesses trying to sell similar products. At the other end, there are very few firms, so there may be less competition. By joining together, businesses are moving along the spectrum. In some cases they may become one of a few oligopolists.

However they play it, they are trying to manage the competitiveness of the market.

PRODUCT DIFFERENTIATION

Any product that stands out from the crowd has a greater chance of success, particularly if the market is overcrowded. However a business sets out to differentiate its products, it aims to create a little bit more power than its competitors. Have a look at page 22.

Power may be created because customers:

■ develop a habit

■ like the image of the product.

To achieve this a business needs to research its market and know what customers want. If image is important, a business must always be considering where the market is going next and try to push things along with new products.

A differentiated product creates power and therefore moves a business along the spectrum of competition. Even a small step can result in profits that make a business stand out from the rest.

One business is often the **market leader**. As the name suggests, it leads the way with price changes, innovation and other factors which keep it ahead of the game.

Work it out

1 What advantage does the angel fish have in the market place?

2 How can a business copy the actions of the angel fish?

3 How does such activity affect its position on the spectrum of competition?

4 How does this affect its ability to make a profit?

TOO MUCH POWER?

A move too far along the spectrum may create so much power that the government starts to worry about the effect on customers. If a merger or takeover threatens to have this effect, it may be referred to the Competition Commission which will decide whether it can go ahead.

Want to find out more?

Who is affected by business power?
See **Who's affected?** page 26.

Controlling monopoly power – the Competition Commission
See **Under control?** page 44.

Who's affected?

ELECTRONICS PLANT
COMES TO
SUNDERLAND

Competition from abroad shuts clothing factory

What's it all about?

You need to understand how competition affects stakeholders in the market – customers, employees, creditors, shareholders, suppliers and the community.

Work it out

1 How has competition brought about these two events?

2 How are customers, employees, suppliers, creditors, shareholders and the community affected in each case?

3 Why do you think people running businesses are concerned about the effect their actions have on the stakeholders?

WHAT IS A STAKEHOLDER?

Quite simply, a stakeholder is someone who has an interest in a business. All the groups in the diagram are affected, one way or another, by the actions of the business.

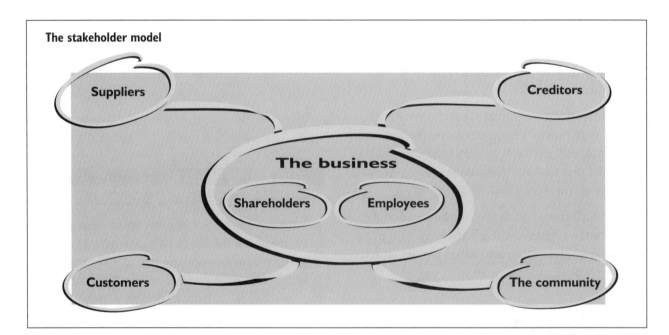

The stakeholder model

Suppliers · Creditors · The business · Shareholders · Employees · Customers · The community

Want to find out more?

Who is affected by business power?
See **Good or bad?** page 42.

Controlling monopoly power – the Competition Commission
See **Under control?** page 44.

THE IMPACT OF BUSINESS

Stakeholder	Impact of business
Customers	Customers are affected by the price, quality, service and availability of products. If a business loses its customers it is in deep trouble so looking after them is a priority. Making sure that the product is just what the customer wants is therefore important. This will involve development work to keep it up to date.
Employees	Employees are often at the mercy of their employers. They are protected by legislation about health and safety, the minimum wage and conditions of employment but the attitude of employers can still affect the way people work. Many businesses value their employees and ensure that they are well motivated and looked after in order to keep them, as it is expensive to recruit and train people. A well-motivated workforce is often more efficient.
Suppliers	Businesses can work closely with suppliers to achieve an efficient, streamlined relationship. Suppliers are generally expected to keep prices as low as possible in order to ensure that the end product is competitive. If this proves impossible, a supplier often loses the contract.
Creditors	Creditors have lent money to the business and expect a return. If they do not receive as much as expected because the business is not making sufficient money, they will want to take their money out. If the business goes under, they will lose their money.
Shareholders	Shareholders own a share of the business. They expect to receive a dividend in return for the money they have put into the business. Shareholders in small businesses will often put up with low returns because they are involved in the business. Shareholders in public companies will quickly pull out in search of a better return if things are not going well. Increasing shareholder value is therefore a top priority for a public company.
The community	The community can be affected by the activities of a business. This can be negative because of pollution, traffic congestion or unemployment. It can also be positive when the business is involved in supporting and working with the community. This is referred to as developing a 'licence to operate' as it demonstrates a commitment to the community.

BAD BEHAVIOUR!

Reputation can be worth millions of pounds and can quickly be lost. When things go wrong, it can take a long time to re-establish the same public attitude to the business. Even an accident, such as the pollution of Perrier water, can be hard to recover from. A mishap in the bottling plant led to cleaning products getting into the water. Despite a rapid clearing of the shelves, customers took a while to return to their previous buying habits.

When a business acts in a way that appears to infringe human rights, a reputation can be damaged for a long period. Some people will not buy Shell petrol because of its activities in Nigeria. Gap and Nike have been challenged for the employment practices of their suppliers in the developing world.

To overcome this, many big companies have set up monitoring systems which are run by outside organisations. Their reports are made public in order to try to reassure their customers.

Work it out

1 Take a look at a newspaper and see how many stories you can find which explore the relationship between a business and its stakeholders.

2 What impact does a bad relationship with each of its stakeholders have on a business?

3 If things go wrong with the relationship, what can a business do to put it right?

Testing times: AQA

The following questions are adapted from AQA tests.

Assessment evidence	
E1	Correct identification of the market and sector of industry within which businesses operate
E2	A recognition and description of characteristics of the market within which businesses operate
E3	An understanding of market conditions that affect the way businesses operate
C2	Analysis of how market conditions might affect businesses and stakeholders
C3	Show why businesses would seek to influence market conditions
A1	An evaluation of the benefits and drawbacks to businesses operating in specific markets
A2	Proposals and justification for appropriate action that businesses could take when faced with changes in policy

1 **For each of the following businesses, identify whether the business operates in the primary, secondary or tertiary sector:**

a	**a business that manufactures car parts for Rover**	**1 mark**
b	**a business that transports Rover cars to showrooms**	**1 mark**
c	**a business that extracts oil**	**1 mark**

Assessment evidence: E1

Sorting out the sectors page 6

| **Help!** | A straightforward question testing knowledge. |

| **Answer** |

(a) secondary
(b) tertiary
(c) primary

2 **Rover operates within a competitive market.**
State three characteristics of a competitive market. **3 marks**

| **From the data** | 'Once again, Ford and Vauxhall were the top two selling companies in the UK, with Peugeot, Renault and Vauxhall all pushing ahead of Rover.' |

Assessment evidence: E2

More competitive? page 22

| **Help!** | Competition can take different forms. Try to relate the theory to your knowledge of the car market. This is not essential but shows that you can apply the ideas. |

| **Answer** |

Businesses selling cars compete on price, differentiate their products, look for ways of adding value and work hard to improve quality. There is also a great deal of advertising.

3   Identify three possible reasons for a fall in the price of cars.   3 marks

From the data	'Drivers appear to be delaying buying new cars in the UK because prices are seen as being far higher than elsewhere in Europe.'

Assessment evidence: E3

Help!   This question asks you to show that you understand the relationship between demand and supply.

Answer

The fall in demand for cars is because people are delaying purchasing cars.
Too many cars for sale because of excess capacity in car production in Europe.
Costs might be falling because production is becoming more efficient.

How much to make? page 10
What will they buy? page 12

4   Explain one way in which operating in a competitive market affects Rover's pricing of its cars.   5 marks

From the data	'Once again, Ford and Vauxhall were the top two selling companies in the UK, with Peugeot, Renault and Vauxhall all pushing ahead of Rover.'

Assessment evidence: C2

Help!   This question asks you to show that you understand how demand and supply affect Rover's pricing strategy.

Answer

Because Rover operates in a competitive market, it must ensure that its prices are set at a level that persuades people to buy its cars. Demand-based pricing means that the price set reflects the price that people are prepared to pay. As Rover has been behind its competitors, it may need to take more drastic action in order to tempt customers back. This might mean opting for penetration pricing in order to capture a greater market share or to move surplus stock. This strategy has to be carefully thought about before being adopted. The company needs to ensure that it is covering its costs and will not be threatened with price cutting by its competitors as this would remove the benefit.

More competitive? page 22

5 **Analyse two possible effects on Rover of a fall in the demand for cars.**   **10 marks**

| From the data | 'Industry observers believe Rover could announce losses of more than £600m, but a spokesman for Rover denied such an announcement would be made.' |

Assessment evidence: E3, C2

How much power? page 18

 Help! A spider diagram makes a good starting point for this question. It can stimulate thoughts and allows you to add ideas where they fit in. Think through the parts of the business and consider what will happen. Take two of the ideas and develop a flow diagram. The sequence of events helps you to analyse the effects. The snip from the data starts you off.

Answer

The following outline shows the sequence of events and their impact on the business. You need to put it into sentences.

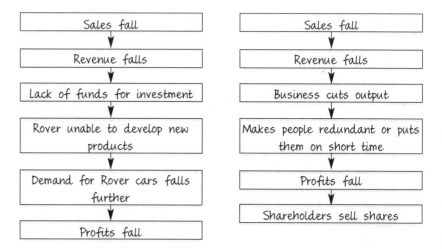

6 **Suggest and justify one policy Rover could take when faced with a fall in demand for their cars.**   **5 marks**

Assessment evidence: A2

More competitive? page 22

 Help! When asked to devise a strategy, make it as realistic as possible. A solution which involves Rover developing a super-car which everyone will want, for example, is not very realistic for a wide range of reasons. The bulk of the marks come from justification, so make sure that you have some good reasons for the policy. To evaluate, you need to put both sides of the argument and come to a conclusion.

Answer

Whichever policy is selected, the relative price of Rover cars and its competitors should be taken into account.

Choose from one of the following:

Cut prices: a policy which will attract more customers, providing the product is one that people want. It should shift cars quite quickly and help the company's cash flow situation. If people like the cars once they have them, it may create a more positive image. If output can be maintained, the plant can continue to work at a reasonable level so employment and staff loyalty are maintained. It might lead to competitive price cutting so the advantage would be lost.

More advertising: this should lead to more sales and therefore improve cash flow. The arguments then follow the same lines as above. The reaction of the competition will affect the success of the policy.

Improve the services associated with the car: by adding value, customers' perception of the cars may change. Providing free services, insurance or including 'extras' in the basic price are all ways in which car companies carry out this strategy. People feel they are getting better value for money, but strategy does not tie Rover to lower prices in the longer run. Its effectiveness will depend on the relative pricing and the extras offered by the competitors. Their responses to the actions of Rover will affect the success of the strategy.

---

7 **Explain why BMW would want to improve the competitiveness of Rover.** **5 marks**

Assessment evidence: C3

 When this question was written, BMW owned Rover. It has since been sold. The question, however, is still valid because it is asking why businesses need to be competitive.

It's a great big market
page 16
More competitive? page 22
Taking power page 24

Answer

BMW wanted Rover to be competitive because it had invested money in the business when it bought it and wanted some return. Unless Rover became more competitive, it would be unable to sell cars on a scale necessary to achieve BMW's financial objectives. If sales are low, Rover's finances will be in trouble. It will be unable to make a return that will keep shareholders happy or provide the resources for investment to improve the range.

A range of cars that is not viewed as competitive by customers has an image problem that is hard to shift. When competitiveness is achieved, the market may not be prepared to accept the change if its perception of Rover is poor value for money.

Testing times: Edexcel

The following questions are adapted from Edexcel tests.

Assessment evidence	
E1	Correct identification of the market and sector of industry within which businesses operate
E2	A recognition and description of characteristics of the market within which businesses operate
E3	An understanding of market conditions that affect the way businesses operate
C2	Analysis of how market conditions might affect businesses and stakeholders
A2	Proposals and justification for appropriate action that businesses could take when faced with changes in market conditions

1 **Clothing and footwear show the greatest increase in expenditure between 1990 and 1998. Explain why this increase is so much greater than the increase for food.**   **4 marks**

From the data   Household final consumption expenditure, by commodity (at 1995 market prices) Non-durable goods (£ billion).

	1990	1992	1994	1996	1998	% change 1990–98
Food	47.1	47.7	48.9	50.9	52.0	10.4
Alcohol and tobacco	41.7	38.4	38.4	38.0	36.4	–12.7
Clothing and footwear	22.1	23.9	27.0	29.8	31.7	43.6
Energy products	27.4	28.0	27.8	28.2	27.6	0.6

Data adapted from: The Annual Abstract of Statistics

The table shows the average household consumption for certain non-durable goods, adjusted for the average rate of inflation.

Assessment evidence: E3

How much to make? page 10

Help!   The question is asking you about how demand changes for different sorts of products. The data takes inflation into account, so it is not asking about the effect of a price rise. It does not tell you about what is happening to income, but it is safe to assume that people grew better off in the period concerned. Think about how increased income affects buying patterns.

Answer

The answer is based on the assumption that people have become better off between 1990 and 1998. Food is an essential part of expenditure, but there is a limit to how much we can eat, so even when people grow richer, their demand for food does not increase significantly. The 10% increase probably comes from an increase in the consumption of prepared foods. If people have more money to spend, they will probably buy more clothing and footwear, as many people like a choice of things to wear.

2 Many durable consumer goods have also experienced very
high increases in expenditure between 1990 and 1998.
Explain, using an example, how you would expect a producer in
such a durable consumer goods market to react to a change
in taste and fashion.   **5 marks**

Assessment evidence: A2

 The question asks you to think about the response of a business making
things like televisions, washing machines and other long lasting products that
are used in the home. There are several ways to answer this question, as a
change of taste might lead to a fall, as well as a rise, in demand. Chose one
line and follow the logic to a conclusion.

Answer

One possible answer is:

The business could carry out some market research to find out
whether the change in taste and fashion is likely to be permanent.
If it suggests that there will be a continued growth in demand,
the business should react accordingly by looking for ways to
increase capacity. Initially, this might mean expanding output
through employing existing staff for longer hours on an overtime
basis. It might be possible to put on a night-shift.

Extra demand could also be met by increasing productivity. This
involves increasing output compared to inputs. The business would
need to look at its production processes in order to achieve this.

If continued growth seems probable, the business might want to
invest in new production capacity.

How much to make? page 10

3 Between 1990 and 1998 the prices of alcohol and tobacco
products have all increased above the rate of inflation.
Referring to the data in question 1, draw a fully labelled supply
and demand graph to show what happened to these products.   **3 marks**

Assessment evidence: E3

 There are two alternative answers to this question. Price may have
increased because demand has risen or supply has fallen. An increase in
demand will shift the demand curve to the right. A fall in supply will shift the
supply curve to the left.

Answer

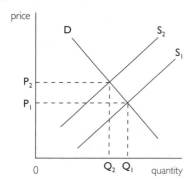

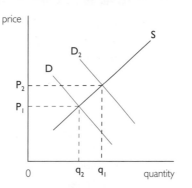

What makes a price? page 8
What will they buy? page 12

HOW COMPETITION IN THE MARKET AFFECTS BUSINESS

33

More competitive? page 22

Taking power page 24

4 Explain how one firm producing gas or electricity could use non-price competition to encourage consumers to buy from its firm rather than from its competitors.   **6 marks**

Assessment evidence: A2

 You need to explain non-price competition and the sort of strategies that a gas or electricity company might use.

Answer

Non-price competition is used by businesses that want to avoid competing on price. An energy company might try to attract customers by offering a better service than its competitors. A promise, for example, that if things go wrong, a fitter will be around the same day is an example of a strategy that might be used. It might also offer free servicing of gas or electrical appliances and updating of meters as technology changes. Advertising may also contribute.

It is hard to differentiate the product itself but by adding value in other ways, customers may be attracted to buy.

5 The holiday industry, and especially selling holidays on the internet, is highly competitive. Your friends (who are setting up a business called Holiweb) have been advised to use penetration pricing.

Briefly explain what penetration pricing is and assess its advantages and disadvantages as a strategy for Holiweb.   **10 marks**

Assessment evidence: A2

More competitive? page 22

Help! The question asks you to define penetration pricing. Then you need to look at both sides of the picture to decide whether it is a good idea for Holiweb. Allocate two marks to the explanation, three marks for each side of the argument and two for summing up.

Answer

Penetration pricing means setting your price below the market price in order to capture customers. It is often used when businesses want to enter a new market. The aim is to capture market share and be a barrier to entry.

For: selling holidays on the web gives customers free access to lots of information, so they are likely to spot your low prices. This will probably lead to a high take-up and many sales. With many sales, you can benefit from economies of scale. You will be able to spread your fixed costs over more sales and may be able to buy hotel rooms etc. more cheaply. As rooms and flights already booked are more likely to be sold, you will also have a higher use of existing capacity.

Against: cut margins so profit is reduced. May be unable to cover costs. If you don't capture more customers, you may not break even. You may not hold the advantage for long because others may retaliate, so no one, except the customers, benefits.

Should Holiweb go ahead? The decision is up to you, as long as you can use the information above as justification. But, as the market is so competitive, it may not be a winning strategy. Others are likely to compete on price as well and, as a new entrant, you may be unable to sustain the low prices. It might be better to look for other ways to be different.

6 In the short run it is likely that an increase in competition will
lead to an increase in Holiweb's costs.

How might this affect two of Holiweb's stakeholders?   **4 marks**

Assessment evidence: C2

Help!   Identify two stakeholders and consider the implications.

Who's affected? page 26

Answer

Choose two of the following:

Owners will suffer if costs rise because customers may buy
holidays elsewhere, so profits will fall.

Customers will be affected by higher prices if costs rise. If prices
are rising across the industry, they will be able to take fewer
holidays.

Suppliers will find that orders fall because of the increases in
costs.

Testing times: OCR

The following questions are adapted from OCR tests.

Assessment evidence	
E1	Correct identification of the market and sector of industry within which businesses operate
E2	A recognition and description of characteristics of the market within which businesses operate
E3	An understanding of market conditions that affect the way businesses operate
C1	Explain how businesses are affected by the type(s) of market within which they operate
C2	Analysis of how market conditions might affect businesses and stakeholders
A2	Proposals and justification for appropriate action that businesses could take when faced with changes in market conditions

1 **Within which sector does British Motors operate?** **1 mark**

From the data	'British Motors is one of the two remaining UK-owned manufacturers of mass-produced motor vehicles.'

Assessment evidence: E1

Sorting out the sectors page 6

Help! A straightforward opening question.

Answer

As British Motors makes cars, it is in the manufacturing or secondary sector.

2 **Describe two characteristics of a market within which few competitors exist.** **6 marks**

From the data	'The market is fiercely competitive with manufacturers looking for new ways of creating competitive advantage.'

Assessment evidence: E2

How much power? page 18

Help! This question can be answered from a theoretical standpoint or by using the evidence. Examples help to show you understand.

Answer

Few competitors may lead to less choice, high prices and non-price competition.

In many industries with few competitors, however, there is keen competition on price. Supermarkets, petrol and airlines all compete on price. The motor industry is described as fiercely competitive.

3 Identify three ways in which current market conditions may
affect British Motors. **6 marks**

From the data	'Some foreign firms have global sales levels ten times greater than those achieved by British Motors.'
	'Rival manufacturers have invested heavily in technology and have improved their productivity significantly. This has, of course, worsened the problem of over-capacity of cars in the European market.'
	'Control over government spending has had an adverse effect on British Motors.'

Assessment evidence: E3, C1

 There is a considerable amount of evidence to help with this question. You
need to think about how it affects British Motors.

Answer

The market is very competitive, so businesses are always looking for
ways to make their products more attractive to customers. They
might add value, for example, by putting the latest CD player into
the car. This has cost implications for the business. Either prices
will be reduced or the costs of each car will rise because
customers are looking for better value. Both of these market
factors will cut profit margins.

There is over-capacity, so more cars are being made than people
want to buy. This will push prices down.

There is pressure to invest in order to make cars more efficiently
and reduce unit prices. British Motors is very small when compared
with competitors, so it has smaller gains from economies of scale.

Demand in the UK has been weak because interest rates have been
higher than elsewhere, so it is more difficult to sell cars.

4 Explain one advantage and one disadvantage to British Motors
resulting from the market structure in which European
motorcar manufacturers trade. **8 marks**

From the data	'Rival manufacturers have invested heavily in technology and have improved their productivity significantly. This has, of course, worsened the problem of over-capacity of cars in the European market.'

Assessment evidence: C1

 This question is asking you to weigh up the situation. The disadvantages are
clearer than the advantages.

Answer

Advantage: a specialist vehicle like the Swift has a role in this
market. Although it is hard to compete in mass-market models,

What makes a price? page 8
How much to make? page 10
Is it tough out there? page 14
Taking power page 24

How much to make? page 10
Is it tough out there? page 14
Taking power page 24

making small numbers of highly regarded sports cars builds a good reputation for the company. It may have a knock-on effect on the image of other vehicles in British Motors' product range as they develop. Potential purchasers may not be as price sensitive as those buying standard small cars.

Disadvantage: British Motors is too small to compete on an equal footing with larger European and global producers. As these companies are selling many more cars, their unit costs are lower because they can invest in the most up-to-date equipment. When producing on a larger scale, a range of activities becomes more viable. Marketing and advertising, for example, is spread over more sales and more potential customers.

---

5 In the role of management consultant you are to conduct an investigation on behalf of the Board of Directors of British Motors. The Board is considering two strategies.

Either concentrating on sports cars and developing the Swift brand
Or merging with another motor car manufacturer

Identify and explain the advantages and disadvantages to:
• the major stakeholders in the company   **8 marks**
• the internal organisation of the business   **8 marks**

From the data	'Withdraw from producing mass-produced cars and concentrate on sports cars, developing the popular Swift brand. This would entail some reductions in the labour force, but would allow a smaller, more efficient company to operate in a market in which its lack of size might be less damaging.'
	'Seek to merge with another major manufacturer. This might provide benefits to both companies and enable the British Motors' name to survive. This would also reflect the recent trends of merger and takeovers within the global motor vehicle industry.'

Assessment evidence: C2, A2

Help! Consider the options and work out the effect on the business and stakeholders. The answer is set out in a table to give a clear pattern. You should write in sentences.

How much to make? page 10

Answer

Stakeholders	Develop the Swift brand	Merger
Shareholders	Uncertainty because success not guaranteed.	Probably a better return if merging with successful competitor.
Suppliers	Orders will be smaller, but if the business is successful, more reliable.	If the business continues on the same basis, a more secure future. If the merger is with a larger company, components may come from its suppliers.
Workforce	Fewer jobs in smaller, specialist business so unemployment.	Bound to be some rationalisation but mass production might continue. New investment involving more automation might also affect employment levels.
Customers	Focus on sports cars will benefit potential customers. Better cars because R&D focused on their future.	Better cars because more resources available for the future. Prices may fall because production more efficient.
Community	If unemployment results, the knock-on effects on the local community may be serious. A successful smaller business, however, may have pay-offs for the community.	If more jobs are preserved, impact less severe.

Effects on internal business

	Swift	Merger
Production	Focused activity setting up lines designed to produce sports cars.	Continued mass production becoming integrated with partner.
Finance	Little change as the business will still be one entity.	Financial systems will have to develop in order to incorporate the two businesses.
Administration	A smaller activity as the business will be reduced in size.	Streamlining as activities will be duplicated in each business.
Marketing	Activity will have a clear focus as it will be selling products to one segment of the market.	Development of a marketing strategy designed to meet the needs of the bigger company. Greater potential, as marketing is often designed with Europe in mind, rather than individual countries.

Testing times: practice questions

In the test, you will be asked to use the ideas that you have learnt to explain how a business works in the market place. To do this well, you need to practise. These questions aim to help you do this. Base your answers on a business you know or a well known company. Whatever the business, work out a really practical answer. Don't just make a list of the theory. If a question doesn't apply to *your* business, think of another business to use.

Business is all around us. To help in your studies, take note of a business in your everyday life, in the papers or on the television. Even the 'soaps' are full of business stories.

1 Does the business sell products, services, or both?

2 Which sector or sectors is the business in?

3 Who buys the products or services?

4 How do demand and supply side factors affect the business?

5 Identify the factors that affect supply in the business.

6 Is anything changing? What effect do these changes have on the supply curve?

7 Identify the factors that affect demand.

8 Is anything changing? What effect do these changes have on the demand curve?

9 Has the price of the product changed recently? Why do you think this has happened?

10 Where does the business sell its products?

11 Does the business face a lot of competition?

12 How does the business compete in the market place? Does it capture a large share of the market with its methods?

13 Are there any factors which make it hard to compete? If so, what are they and how do they affect the business?

14 What might the business do when faced with changes in the market place?

15 If the business wanted to win a bigger share of the market, what might it do?

16 If the business has a very large share of the market, what effect might it have on its decisions about price? Why?

17 Who are the stakeholders of the business?

18 What effect does the business have on the stakeholders?

19 What effect do the stakeholders have on the business?

20 What would you do to make the business bigger and/or better?

How business is affected by government policy

Good or bad?

What's it all about?

You need to understand why the government intervenes to influence the effect business has on stakeholders.

WIELDING POWER

Businesses can affect stakeholders in all sorts of ways. Generally it is for the good. People receive good quality products at a price that doesn't exploit the customer. Sometimes things go wrong, either by accident or by design.

- Businesses may not look after their employees well. Sometimes people are expected to work in poor conditions, without holidays or for low pay. People may be unfairly sacked or not have proper contracts of employment. Everyone is protected from these activities by law. The legislation is there because an individual is often in too weak a position to challenge an employer who has acted unfairly.

- Businesses may be in a position to take advantage of consumers. It may happen because marketing material is misleading and the product does not match up. This may be deliberate or done unwittingly, but the effect is still the same.

Work it out

1 Which stakeholders are affected by the activities shown here?

2 How are they affected?

3 Why is it sometimes important for the government to intervene to control business?

- Sometimes a salesman may use heavy pressure to persuade a customer to buy, especially when the amount involved is large.

- Businesses may have too much power because the market they are in is not very competitive. If so, prices may be set high as customers have little alternative.

- Businesses may pollute the environment because it keeps production costs low. If they were to install equipment to clean up the waste, there would be extra costs, so the products would be less competitive.

The government is anxious to protect consumers from these activities. All sorts of legislation controls the way businesses behave.

Laws about	What does it do?
Employees	Protects against unfair dismissal Ensures a healthy and safe working environment Ensures fair conditions of employment Ensures a minimum wage
Consumers	Protects against faulty products Protects against incorrect claims Protects against heavy pressure on credit sales Controls the way food is sold
Competition	Prevents businesses from exploiting monopoly power by putting up prices or limiting supply
Environment	Prevents businesses polluting rivers, air, sea and land

WHY ARE THERE LAWS?

A business which just wants to make a profit will try to keep costs as low as possible.

- If sales fall, for example, it might sack people at short notice.

- Poor quality materials will be cheaper but might not be safe.

- Worn out equipment might be unsafe but expensive to replace.

Some businesses may try to cut corners in order to stay competitive. One of the few ways to control such behaviour is to pass laws that limit these activities. By making businesses look after their staff and ensuring that products are safe, costs of production will rise, but everyone is in the same boat. Within the UK and Europe everyone is on an equal footing as EU legislation covers most of these areas.

Some countries do not have the same standards, and issues arise when cheap products are imported from countries where it is not essential to look after staff or keep pollution to a minimum.

AN ALTERNATIVE

For some activities, legislation may prove impossible because the actions take place overseas or because it is difficult to monitor. Industries that want to protect their image often set up a system of self-regulation. This occurs more often in fields in which ethical judgements are made. When a business hits the headlines for its actions, it is well aware of the impact it may have on sales.

Want to find out more?

The Competition Commission
    See **Under control?** page 44.

Consumer protection
    See **Looking after the customer** page 46.

Environmental protection and ethical issues
    See **In need of help?** page 48.

Under control?

'Oh sorry, we don't keep Saturns. Doors won't let us put other companies' ice cream in their fridge.'

Work it out

1 Why does Doors have this rule?

2 Why would the maker of Saturns be unhappy about Doors' policy?

3 How is the customer affected by Doors' policy?

COMPETITION RULES OK!

Competition leads to consumers having more choice, fairer prices and, generally, a better deal. Businesses are often trying to find ways to reduce competition as this can make life easier.

Some strategies are very acceptable. Making your product a little different so people will choose it in favour of others is fine. Restricting the activities of other businesses is not. There are laws against it.

The Competition Act of 1998 replaced previous competition legislation and brought the UK into line with Europe.

The Act outlaws anti-competitive agreements and any abuse of a dominant position. In other words, one powerful business, or a group which gets together to prevent others from competing is banned from taking advantage of their position.

They might be tempted to fix prices or allocate market shares amongst themselves rather than by competing. Fixing retail prices also contravenes the rules.

The example of the ice cream fridges is one that has been dealt with in the past.

THE WATCHDOG

The **Office of Fair Trading** (OFT) is the organisation that monitors business behaviour in the field of competition. It has the power to investigate any anti-competitive activities that come to its attention. Have a look at its website at www.oft.gov.uk

If the business has infringed the rules, it can be ordered to stop. It might also be liable for a fine, equivalent to 10% of its UK turnover.

The OFT also monitors mergers and takeovers because they can reduce competition. There will be an informal investigation to decide whether there is a threat to competition and if a threat seems likely, the merger or takeover will be referred to the **Competition Commission**.

CONTROLLING MONOPOLY POWER

The Competition Commission (CC) carries out inquiries when asked by the OFT or the regulators of the utility companies. If two water companies want to merge, for example, it might be referred to the CC. Have a look at its website at www.competition-commission.org.uk

The Commission will investigate if a merger would lead to:

- a business controlling more than 25% of the market;

- the acquisition of more than £70 million gross assets.

It may come to the conclusion that the merger is '**in the public interest**'. This means, for example, that costs would be reduced by the merger so customers would benefit. If, however, it seems to put too much power into the hands of one company, it may not be allowed.

Sometimes a business is told to sell off some subsidiary businesses in order to reduce the proportion of market share that it controls. After doing so, the merger can go ahead. The Competition Commission website has recent examples of inquiries that it has carried out.

IF YOU RUN A BUSINESS...

You must not

- agree to fix purchase or selling prices

- agree to limit or control production, markets, technical development or investment

- agree to share markets or sources of supply

- agree to apply different trading conditions to the same transactions with different people, therefore placing some people at a disadvantage

- agree to make contracts subject to unrelated conditions

or the Office of Fair Trading will be after you!

Work it out

1 Why is controlling anti-competitive activities so important?

2 If other countries control such practices but the UK doesn't, what effect might it have on our business?

3 Search a newspaper website for examples of mergers that are taking place. Has the Competition Commission been asked to investigate?

4 Find a case, either in the papers or on the Competition Commission website, in which a business has contravened the rules. What was the problem?

The Competition Commission told Interbrew that it must sell Bass. One of the reasons was ...

'As a result of the merger, Interbrew and S&N would have the largest and most efficient wholesaling and distribution operations in Great Britain. While competing brewers may be able to rely on the centralized wholesaling and distribution arrangements offered by some multiple retailers, this will not enable entrants or smaller brewers to access either multiple retailers that do not offer such services or the independent free trade. For these customers, Interbrew and S&N would effectively control the route to market.'

Source: Competition Commission website

Looking after the customer

What's it all about?

You need to know the ways in which government acts to protect customers.

'But I only asked for a cut!!!'

'I followed the washing instructions.'

Work it out

1 What would you do in these circumstances?
2 Do you have 'right' on your side?
3 Find out below, how the law will help you.

WATCH OUT – THERE'S A LAW ABOUT!

If you are selling products or services to the public, it is essential to be aware of the laws that affect your business. They are designed to protect customers from unacceptable business behaviour.

Anything you sell must be:

■ of satisfactory quality

The quality of the product must be acceptable. Louis Vuitton luggage is a popular choice of the rich and famous. It costs thousands of pounds and is expected to be a delight to look at as well as functioning well. A suitcase that costs £25 may not be quite so glamorous but it still must serve the purpose and not fall apart at its first trip on EasyJet. Anything sold should be acceptable when the price and description are taken into account.

■ fit for the purpose

If you are aware that the customer wants to buy a piece of software for an Apple computer and you sell one for a PC, it is not 'fit for the purpose'. If they want boots to trek across Africa and you sell ones that can hardly cope with an afternoon stroll, they are not 'fit for the purpose'. If they are brought back, you will be expected to replace them.

■ as described

If packaging or marketing material makes claims about the product, the contents must live up to them. Leather shoes must not prove to be plastic. A diamond ring cannot be glass.

IF YOU ARE SELLING A SERVICE, IT'S JUST THE SAME

Whatever the service, a customer is entitled to a standard of care. Any service must be provided:

■ **with reasonable care and skill**

If you are repairing cars, workmanship must be of a good standard. If the brakes are being fixed, they must work when the car leaves your garage.

■ **within a reasonable time**

When no one has discussed how long a job will take, a customer should expect it to be finished in a reasonable time.

■ **at a reasonable charge, if no price has been fixed in advance**

It's best to fix a price in advance. The customer cannot complain that it is unreasonable if they accepted it. If costs are rising, it should be discussed and agreed before further work is done.

☞ **Law: Sales of Goods Act 1979**
   Trade Description Act 1968

EVERYTHING YOU SELL MUST BE SAFE

Whatever the product, it has to be safe, even if it is second hand. If you sell things that are unsafe, expect a visit from the local Trading Standards Department. They will have some tricky questions for you to answer. The only exceptions are antiques and things that are clearly stated to be in need of repair.

☞ **Law: Consumer Protection Act 1987**
   Food Safety Act 1990

EVEN IF THERE'S A CONTRACT ...

A contract is a legal agreement between two people. There are, however, rules about what can be in a contract. Unfair Contract Terms means that you cannot include clauses which limit the consumer's right in unacceptable ways – in exclusion clauses for example.

■ You cannot vary the terms of the contract if the customer can't.

■ You can't withdraw from a contract if the customer can't.

■ The customer can insist on holding back part of the payment until they are satisfied.

■ You can't dishonour a promise made by one of your sales staff.

■ You can't prevent a customer going to court if there is a dispute.

☞ **Law: Unfair Contract Terms Act 1995**

Work it out

You had a conservatory built but:

❑ the salesman offered an extra special deal but the company denied all knowledge of it;

❑ the company wanted you to pay before they began;

❑ they tried to pull out once you had signed on the dotted line;

❑ they came up with an exorbitant bill for extra work that was needed;

❑ the supplier finished months after the expected date;

❑ it let in water.

You might wish you had never begun, but which laws would help you to deal with these situations?

In need of help?

What's it all about?

You need to know how and why the government becomes involved in environmental, social and ethical issues.

Work it out

1 What sort of things cause global warming?

2 Find out, from the information below, how the government and the EU is dealing with it.

3 How does this affect business?

4 How is business affected if some countries take the problem more seriously than others?

A SUSTAINABLE FUTURE?

Global warming has a variety of causes but mainly stems from carbon dioxide emissions. Governments of the developed world assemble at intervals to set targets to reduce these and other emissions. These targets are met with varying degrees of success.

WHY?

The potential damage from global warming seems almost beyond measure. By controlling it we can minimise the damage, if not completely reverse it, so the government takes a variety of steps to stop businesses from causing problems.

If businesses behave badly in environmental, social or ethical ways, their costs are often reduced, but someone else ends up with the bill. This may be the government or the individuals concerned. People have been killed by asbestos in buildings, and miners have died from the effect of breathing air full of coal dust. The individuals have suffered and been unable to work. The government has had to pay for more health care.

GUIDANCE OR CONTROL?

The government takes two approaches in its plans to improve the environment. Much is done by providing guidance to help businesses to behave better. The alternative is to throw the weight of the law behind the problem. On some occasions, **subsidies** are given to businesses to encourage them to supply products in a particular way or produce things that might not have been made otherwise.

Guidance

The Department of Transport, the Environment and the Regions website is full of advice for businesses about reducing the impact they have on the environment. Here are two examples of the sort of assistance available.

- Government runs an environmental helpline for small and medium sized businesses. There is free advice on the phone from experts or a site visit for smaller businesses.

- Have a look at guidance of the Advisory Committee on Business and the Environment http://www.environment.detr. gov.uk/acbe/directors/01.htm to find out how the directors of a business should be thinking about environmental, social and ethical issues.

If you want to explore further go to www.detr.gov.uk

The law

Legislation affects businesses in different ways. Emissions into the air, rivers, sea and on to the land are controlled. Failure to keep the rules leads to a fine, although sometimes the fines are not big enough to deter poor practice.

Other strategies include the banning of new out-of-town shopping centres, for example. This aims to reduce the use of the car, but also has social implications because it helps to retain the local high street as a viable economic unit.

Plans for road pricing are emerging. This will discourage car use, reduce congestion and therefore have a positive impact on the environment in several ways.

All these strategies aim to help the UK to meet the EU's targets on the environment. The table on the right shows how well EU countries are doing.

THE BUSINESS RESPONSE

If the first responsibility of a business is to pay its shareholders a good dividend, spending money on environmentally-sound activities may seem to be foolish. If shareholders sell up, the value of the business will fall. Many large businesses have, however, recognised that this is not the case.

Customers are often loyal to a business which they feel has a sense of responsibility, so shareholders and other stakeholders can all be winners.

The government can only enforce social and ethical responsibility through employment law, planning regulations and other types of regulations. Many businesses go much further and carry out extensive social and environmental audits to identify what they are doing well, and where there is room for improvement. The Co-op Bank has built its whole image on its ethical stance.

You will find evidence of these audits on many of the major public companies' websites. Try www.bp.com, www.bodyshop.com or www.unilever.com

Work it out

1 How does a business you know deal with environmental, social or ethical issues?

2 How does its actions help the business and its stakeholders?

Emissions of carbon dioxide: EU comparison, 1990 and 1998

Million tonnes	1990	1998	% change 1990–1998
Luxembourg	13	5	–61
Germany	1015	886	–13
United Kingdom	584	544	–7
Sweden	55	57	3
France	388	413	7
Italy	430	458	7
Belgium	114	122	7
Austria	62	67	7
Finland	59	64	8
Netherlands	161	181	12
Denmark	53	60	14
Greece	85	100	18
Spain	226	273	21
Portugal	43	54	25
Irish Republic	32	40	26

Source: Social Trends 2001, ONS

Government business?

What's it all about?

You need to be able to explain how businesses are affected by policies towards public sector services.

'Well, which ones will make money?'

Work it out

1. How will Speedy Trains make money from running a rail service?
2. Why do you think the government wants businesses to run the services?
3. What difficulties might arise for the customer, the business and the government?

RUNNING THE BUSINESS

Governments used to run all sorts of businesses themselves. Coal, steel, cars and power generation have all been in the hands of government. All have now been privatised. Shares were sold to the public when they became public limited companies.

The government has dealt with businesses that it used to run in a range of ways as it does not want to lose control completely. Some of these activities were in the hands of local government as well as national government.

Strategy	Industry	Control
Privatisation	Water, telephones, power generation	Regulators: Ofwat, Oftel, Ofgen, control prices
Tendering	Railways, lottery, school dinners and cleaning	Threat of loss of contract at end of a set time period
Deregulation	Buses	Health and safety rules and Office of Fair Trading

PROVIDING OPPORTUNITIES

The change in government policy in the last twenty years has created opportunities for businesses in areas that were confined to government control. Some businesses have specialised in winning contracts from public sector organisations. Some are eligible for **subsidies**. These are special grants from the government to help them provide services in areas where there would be no profit. Businesses would obviously not be prepared to run them without such help.

At a national level, the supply of train services is the key example. In order to maintain quality, contracts are granted for a limited period. If a company fails to meet targets or if others offer a better deal, its contract will not be renewed. Connex, for example, lost a contract to run trains in SE England.

At a local level, buses work on the same principle. You may notice that the company running your local bus service changes from time to time. Many other local services are contracted out.

- Schools and hospitals have services that are contracted out.

- Refuse collection is frequently run by a company in place of the local council.

- All residential care is in private hands. Care homes are registered and inspected. The local authority then buys their services.

UNDER CONTROL?

Some people criticise the degree of control over businesses running these services. Issues arise when things go wrong. There may be no immediate redress but the company providing the service will be aware that there is no guaranteed future if they are unsuccessful.

The uncertainty of the system can lead to businesses being unwilling to invest. Even if a contract lasts five years, by the time investment plans are made and carried out, there may be little time left to recoup the outlay.

Public/private partnerships are also a way of bringing in investment, while keeping a government finger in the pie. The debate over London's underground network has revolved around whether this is the best strategy.

IN GOVERNMENT HANDS

The Post Office is still run by the government, although it has been turned into a company called Consignia. It has been given greater flexibility so that it can compete more effectively in national and international markets.

The need for a fair system for mail delivery has been one of the main factors for the retention of the Post Office in the public sector. Delivering mail in towns is cheap, but providing the service in remote rural areas is expensive. There is a fear that a private sector organisation would want to charge differential rates in order to meet the costs.

Work it out

1 Find out who runs the catering and cleaning in your school or college. How are they monitored?

2 If it is run by a company, what other contracts does it have?

3 What opportunities does this system provide for local businesses?

4 Why is quality control an issue?

A slice of the cake

What's it all about?

You need to be able to explain how businesses are affected by policies towards taxation.

WHY TAX?

If the government is going to have money to spend on things the country needs and expects, it has to raise it somehow. **Taxation** is the answer. Many people complain about paying taxes but without them the country would be short of many of the necessities we need for business to function efficiently.

WHAT DOES BUSINESS PAY?

Companies pay:

- Corporation tax: a percentage of profits.

Other taxes are paid by businesses and people alike:

Work it out

1 Where does the money come from to build the bypass?

2 What would life be like if no one paid taxes?

3 Why might the government want to increase taxes?

4 What effect would this have on business?

- Social Security payments for staff: a percentage of wages;

- Value Added Tax: a percentage of the price;

- car tax;

- petrol duty and all the other forms of taxation on consumption.

WHAT DO THEY GET FOR THEIR MONEY?

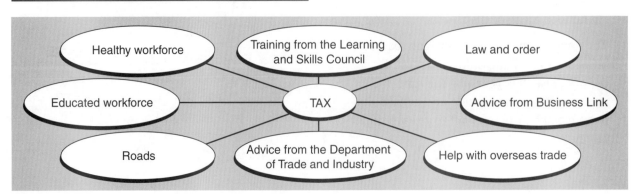

Going up

If the government raises taxes, it takes money out of customers' pockets and therefore reduces demand for the output of business. The government may have good reasons. Perhaps it wants to limit spending before the economy starts to grow too fast, or perhaps it wants to give more to the poor.

The reason will affect the outcome.

■ If the government wants to redistribute income to improve the lot of the poor, consumers will buy more basic products, like food and clothes, but fewer luxury goods as the rich will have less to spend. The effects will therefore differ from business to business.

■ If the government simply wants to cut spending, businesses may be affected across the board, although those supplying basic needs are likely to be less severely affected.

Going down

If the government cuts taxes, people have more to spend. This doesn't help all businesses because the customers may upgrade their spending. Instead of buying bottom-grade coffee, they might move to a better quality product. As the poorest do not pay tax, the impact on basic consumption will be limited.

Tax can be used as a means of persuading individuals and businesses to buy or produce more of some things than others. As most people are price-sensitive to some extent, increasing the price by taxing a product will reduce consumption. Taxing one product less than another that performs the same function will help people to decide between the two.

Incentives

Leaded petrol has just about disappeared but its demise was decided when the government lowered the tax on unleaded petrol. People didn't want cars that would be more expensive to run. Taxation was being used to clean up the environment. The motor industry had to adjust to meet the new situation.

Disincentives

The amount of tax on cigarettes, beer, wine, spirits and petrol are all aimed at reducing consumption. Of course, the Chancellor of the Exchequer still enjoys the flow of income that it gives him. The pie chart shows how tax revenue is spent in an average year.

The cigarette industry has been badly affected as the combination of high prices and bad press has reduced demand considerably.

How the Government spends its money

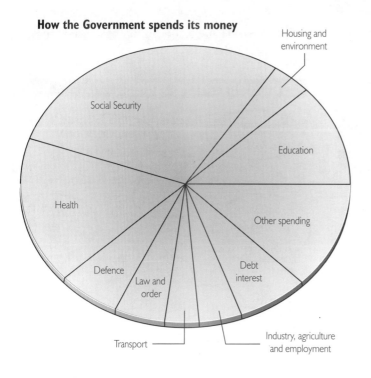

Work it out

1 How do changes in government policy on tax affect businesses?

2 How will Rolls Royce, BHS, Quicksave, Luis Vuitton, Matalan, VW and PC World each be affected by
   (a) an increase in taxes?
   (b) a cut in taxes?

Going up?

'But it was £20 less last week.'

'I know – prices keep going up at the moment.'

What's it all about?

You need to be able to analyse the impact on business of government policies for controlling inflation.

Work it out

1 Why do customers not like prices going up?
2 Why do businesses not like prices going up?
3 If prices are going up, what may people start demanding of their employers?
4 What effect does this have on business?

BUSINESSES AND INFLATION

Businesses don't like **inflation** much. When prices are rising over a period of time, it means that they don't know:

■ what inputs will cost in future

or

■ the price at which they can sell the output.

It causes uncertainty, especially if the business is involved in international trade. If inflation is higher in the UK than in other countries, prices will be rising more quickly. This makes UK products less attractive overseas and sales may fall.

If a business relies on imports to make its product it will benefit as everything will become cheaper.

Whether a winner or loser, it still creates uncertainly and this makes planning hard.

THE COSTS TO BUSINESS

New price lists

New labels on shelves

Employees pressing for higher pay

Inflation

Search for cheaper sources

Updating computer systems

Competition from overseas

THE ROLE OF GOVERNMENT

Economies tend to go through cycles of boom and slump. This is commonly called the **Business Cycle**. In a **boom**, inflation tends to be a problem as people want more of everything and a shortage of supply increases prices. Have a look at pages 8 and 9 to refresh your memory on demand and supply.

In a **slump** or **recession**, which is a less severe form of slump, unemployment is the main problem because people do not want to buy all that the country can produce.

Governments work hard to reduce the effects of the business cycle because it is very disruptive for all economic activity.

CONTROLLING INFLATION

In recent years, inflation has been relatively stable in the UK. A committee of the Bank of England, known as the **Monetary Policy Committee** has been given the task of adjusting **interest rates**, the cost of borrowing money, on a monthly basis in order to keep inflation under control. This has separated the decision from government.

An approaching election often tempts the ruling party to make everyone feel good by putting more money into their pockets. Cutting interest rates would have this effect but it might cause inflation in the future.

As interest rates are the cost of borrowing

money, a cut will reduce the payments on any loans. Many people in the UK have mortgages to buy houses. These are often large. If interest rates are cut, repayments on the mortgage can fall significantly. This releases money for people to spend on other things. Many businesses will be very happy as a result!

But – there is always a but – if everyone has more to spend, prices will start to rise in the end as there will be a limit to how much businesses can produce. This is when inflation begins.

The Monetary Policy Committee has to tread a fine line between preventing inflation and pushing the economy into recession. It looks in detail at all the changes happening in the economy and makes its decision.

In countries which are members of the euro, interest rate decisions are made centrally.

Governments can also use **taxation** to control inflation. It has the same effect of changing the amount of money that people have in their pockets and can be more selective according to the taxes which are changed.

WHAT ABOUT GOVERNMENT SPENDING?

If the government cuts spending, it takes money out of the economy. This is another strategy for controlling inflation. In a recession, the government may spend more, in order to put money into people's pockets.

Controlling inflation

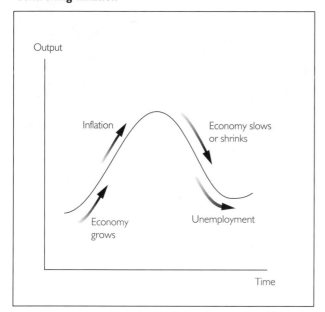

Work it out

1 Why do governments want to control inflation?

2 What effect does inflation have on businesses?

3 What effect can interest rates have on the sales of a business?

Want to find out more?

The impact of changing interest rates on business
See **Borrow – at a price?** page 60.

What's happened to the jobs?

What's it all about?

You need to be able to analyse the impact on business of government policies for controlling unemployment.

WHY DOES THE GOVERNMENT INTERVENE?

Unemployment, the number of people who are seeking work, tends to move up and down with the business cycle. In times of boom, most people are employed. In times of recession, the number falls. In mild recessions, it falls a little but if recession turns to slump, the situation can become very serious.

Work it out

1 What problem does this situation pose for business?

2 How can the government help to overcome it?

3 How can business help to overcome it?

4 What are the drawbacks for business of millions of people being unemployed?

The downward spiral of unemployment

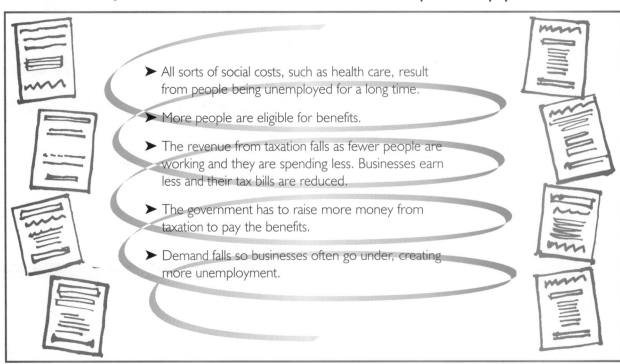

➤ All sorts of social costs, such as health care, result from people being unemployed for a long time.

➤ More people are eligible for benefits.

➤ The revenue from taxation falls as fewer people are working and they are spending less. Businesses earn less and their tax bills are reduced.

➤ The government has to raise more money from taxation to pay the benefits.

➤ Demand falls so businesses often go under, creating more unemployment.

The government tries to manage unemployment levels as it tries to manage inflation. The strategy required aims to match the cause.

A **skills mismatch** can lead to unemployment, even in times of growth. The government has a variety of strategies which aim to overcome the problem. The Learning and Skills Council is responsible for all post-16 education and training. It is their responsibility to work with business to identify regional training needs and plan provision.

Business Link is a government-funded advisory body for small and medium sized businesses. It provides guidance as to needs, and how to plan for skills development.

The shortage of skills in some sectors can prevent businesses growing as quickly as they might. The government, therefore, has two agendas in helping people to develop skills:

■ to retrain the unemployed;

■ to prevent growing businesses running short of skilled people.

Regional decline can lead to some parts of the country suffering high levels of unemployment while others are growing quickly. This occurs mainly in areas that had heavy industry such as the north-east, north-west and South Wales. There are many people who have skills that are no longer required and need retraining. Before this can begin, new businesses need to be attracted to the area. Grants and loans are available in such areas in order to help people to set up there. They are often used to attract and keep foreign investment in such regions. This has to be done with care because the EU is concerned that governments do not give more money than would be available in other countries.

Both government and private developments help to create jobs. If more people are working, more people are spending so it is good for businesses in the area. Despite the fact that in many ways the Millennium Dome was a disaster, it brought jobs and money to Greenwich, one of London's poorest areas.

Recession generally affects the whole country but often some regions are affected more severely than others. The government may choose to cut taxation in order to give people more to spend, but more often it relies on the changes in interest rate to make the difference. Cutting interest rates gives people more to spend. Each month when the Monetary Policy Committee meets at the Bank of England, the members are asked to consider changes in the number of people employed before they come to their decision.

Any strategy which is used to make people better off will help business as everyone will have more to spend.

Employment rates by area

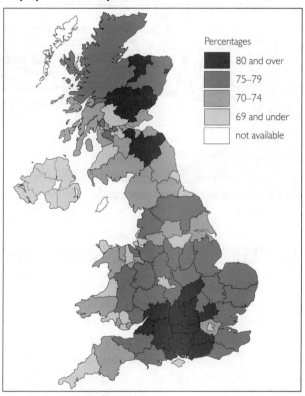

Source: *Social Trends 2001, ONS*

Work it out

1 Why is a lack of people with the right skills damaging to businesses, particularly those which trade with other countries?

2 How will training more people help business?

3 Draw a spider diagram showing how the Millennium Dome, or a major project near you, has helped local business.

4 Why does putting more money into people's pockets help business and the economy? Draw a flow diagram to show what happens.

HOW BUSINESS IS AFFECTED BY GOVERNMENT POLICY

Who's getting richer?

What's it all about?

You need to be able to analyse the impact on business of government policies concerning growth.

'People want the products but how can we produce enough?'

Work it out

1 What are they going to need to do to increase production?

2 What problems might they encounter?

3 How might the government help them to achieve the objective of growth?

WHAT IS GROWTH?

A growing economy results from all the businesses in the country producing more. By adding up all their output, you can see how much the economy has grown. This is generally known as **Gross Domestic Product** or GDP. *Real* GDP shows you what's *really* happening as it takes inflation into account. This means that you can compare the value from one year to the next. The government produces data to show what has been happening. You can see for yourself at www.statistics.gov.uk

Growth in a business comes from:

■ raising **productivity**, which means increasing output compared to inputs. To do this, existing resources must be used more efficiently;

■ **investment**, which means putting more resources into the business. It may mean new buildings or machinery but can also meaning investing in training, so people can use new techniques.

WHAT DOES THE GOVERNMENT DO?

The government faces two challenges:

■ to keep the business cycle under control

■ to help the country to become more competitive.

Policies relating to both of these can help businesses grow.

INFLUENCING THE BUSINESS CYCLE

Measures to influence inflation on pages 54–55 and unemployment on pages 56–57 affect businesses in a variety of ways.

In a boom, the government wants to slow the economy down to prevent inflation so it tries to cut demand. This will affect businesses by reducing demand for products and services. Although this seems tough, it is a long-run strategy because letting the economy rip may result in a crash with high unemployment and lots of businesses going under. We have already seen how the government tries to reduce inflation (see *Want to find out more?*).

Another strategy is to help businesses grow to meet demand. It can, for example, help business find the employees that it needs to increase output, so that prices do not rise to the same extent.

In a recession, the government wants to help the economy grow by cutting interest rates to increase demand. This will create employment and therefore increase demand further. It might also use the tax system to help (see *Want to find out more?*). Training people with the right skills for the jobs market also helps.

When the economy is in recession it is often hard to persuade businesses to take risks. As running a business is all about risk taking, it is not a healthy environment, so encouragement is often needed. The incentives below are often used in association with interest rate policy.

Moderating the business cycle

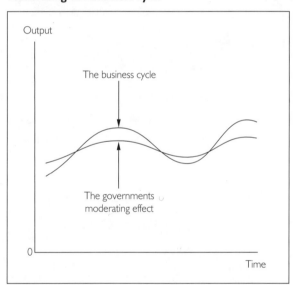

INCREASING COMPETITIVENESS

In a highly competitive world market, countries have to find ways of improving their efficiency if growth is the objective. This is often done through offering carrots, or incentives, such as:

■ training programmes to overcome skills shortages;

■ cutting the cost of employing people, by reducing the social security contribution paid by business;

■ increased flexibility in employment law, so businesses can hire and fire more easily;

■ reducing red tape, so small businesses can concentrate on production;

■ encouraging research and development, so businesses can add more value;

■ encouraging people to work by reducing tax rates at the bottom of the scale, so people are better off working than on benefits.

Sometimes it is necessary to wield a stick to make businesses avoid anti-competitive practices.

■ The Office of Fair Trading and the Competition Commission, on pages 44–45, keep an eye on the activities of businesses. When businesses break the competition laws, they reduce competitiveness because they will not be producing efficiently.

For the latest strategies government is using to help businesses become more competitive, have a look at the website of the Department of Trade of Industry, www.dti.gov.uk

Work it out

1 Why is growth good for business?
2 Why are growing businesses good for the economy?
3 Why is it important for a business to be competitive?
4 If a business wants to grow, how might the government help?
5 Why can growth get too fast?

Want to find out more?

Governments and inflation
    See **Going up?** page 54.

Governments and unemployment
    See **What's happened to the jobs?** page 56.

Borrow - at a price?

What's it all about?

You need to be able to explain how businesses are affected by policies towards changes in interest rates.

Work it out

1 Why might profits be falling if interest rates are rising? Have a look at pages 54–55 if you need some help.

2 If a business has borrowed a lot of money, how will a rise in interest rates affect it?

3 If a business is planning to expand and needs to borrow money, how will a rise in interest rates affect its decision? What effect will this have on economic growth?

4 If interest rates are higher in the UK than elsewhere, what effect might this have on a business involved in international trade?

CUTTING SPENDING

Raising interest rates is a strategy used by the government to cut the amount that people have to spend in order to reduce the risk of rising inflation. If people are being discouraged from spending, businesses will suffer a fall in turnover and profits.

If the policy works, business will gain in the long run because the economy will be more stable. If inflation gets out of control, boom can quickly turn to recession.

PAYING FOR BORROWING

Many businesses borrow money to help them grow and develop. Borrowing decisions are made in the light of the repayments that have to be made and the returns that are expected, among other things. The possibility of increased interest rates should be built into the decision.

The trouble is that plans don't always work perfectly. If sales are not as high as expected, or costs have risen in other ways, an increase in interest rates can put great financial pressures on a business. Sometimes it can be the final straw.

Banks, in the past, have been lax on the amount of money that they lent. The result was that when interest rates started to rise, many businesses went under. Banks set their own interest rates, based on the rate set by the Monetary Policy Committee. As small businesses are thought to be a greater risk than big businesses, they are often charged higher rates of interest, so the pressure on them is greater.

The **gearing** of a business will tell you how vulnerable it is. It shows the relationship between the amount that has been borrowed and the capital employed which is made up of share capital and long-term loans.

$$\frac{\text{Long-term liabilities (loans)}}{\text{Capital employed}} \times 100$$

If a business has lots of borrowing compared with its capital employed it is highly geared, so a rise in interest rates may cause difficulties.

Some businesses use borrowing to keep their heads above water. If working capital is based on borrowed money, the business is probably in serious difficulties.

INVESTING

Many investment decisions are based on borrowed money. If a business is planning to buy a new van or build a new factory, it will look at the rate of interest to help it to decide whether to go ahead. If rates are likely to rise, the return on the investment will need to be higher to cover the cost.

High rates may, therefore, make some plans impractical. What businesses really want is stability.

THE COST OF TRADE

If interest rates are high in the UK compared to other countries, it is harder for businesses to be competitive. Interest rates add to the cost of making things if money has been borrowed.

The international market is very competitive so it will become harder for businesses to sell abroad if rates are high.

All countries which have joined the euro have the same interest rate, so trade between them is on a level playing field. Their concern is the relationship with countries outside the euro. If interest rates are lower elsewhere, international contracts will be harder to win.

Work it out

1 Why does the government want to keep interest rates as low as possible?

2 How are individuals affected by changing interest rates? How does this affect business?

3 Draw a spider diagram showing the effects of rising interest rates on a business.

4 How is a business you know affected by changing interest rates?

High interest rates
- expensive borrowing
  - ❑ needs higher return
- customers have less to spend
  - ❑ needs higher return

Low interest rates
- cheap borrowing for businesses
  - ❑ needs lower return
- cheap borrowing for customers
  - ❑ needs lower return

Shall we invest?

Changing money

What's it all about?

You need to be able to explain how businesses are affected by policies towards exchange rates.

WHAT IS AN EXCHANGE RATE?

When you go to America you change your pounds into dollars. The **exchange rate** is the number of pounds you have to pay to buy those dollars. $100 would cost about £60 so the exchange rate is $1 to £0.60.

You will find the tourist exchange rates in every newspaper. If you keep an eye on them, you will see that they don't stand still. This can cause problems for businesses as it makes their costs and pricing uncertain.

LIVING WITH EXCHANGE RATES

Changes in exchange rates can make life difficult because it causes uncertainty. Prices fluctuate with inflation, and exchange rates add another dimension.

All sorts of things can make exchange rates change. If interest rates are high in the UK, people will want to buy £s to earn good interest. This increases the demand for the pound so you have to pay more dollars or euros to buy them.

Work it out

1 How will changes in the price list from the Brazilian Chocolate Company affect the costs of the Supreme Chocolate Company?

2 If the value of the peso falls so you can buy more with a pound, what will happen to the costs of the Supreme Chocolate Company?

3 If the value of the pound falls, what will happen to costs of UK businesses that import materials?

4 If the value of the pound falls, what will happen to the export price of the products of UK businesses? What will happen to the amount that is exported as a result?

5 If the value of the pound falls, explain the effect on imports and exports.

THE POUND: HIGH OR LOW?

- A **high pound** makes imports cheap

  – so costs will fall for a business that uses imported resources.

- A high pound makes our products expensive to sell abroad

  – so demand may fall for products sold abroad.

When companies are involved in international trade, they may work hard to ensure that they keep the costs of exchanging money low. To do

- A **low pound** makes imports expensive

  – so costs will rise for a business that uses imported resources

- A low pound makes our products cheap abroad

  – so demand may rise for products sold abroad

this they employ people who are experts on exchange rates, and buy and sell currencies to meet their needs.

WHY JOIN THE EURO?

The euro is the common currency of some members of the European Union. In 1999, eleven members decided to join. It means that all the countries use the same currency and therefore do not need to worry about exchange rates for trade within the group.

They don't have to pay banks to change money.

Exchange rates don't affect prices within the member group.

Why do businesses like a common currency?

It removes uncertainty within the member group.

It reduces the costs of dealing with member countries.

Have a look at the Confederation of British Industry's website. It represents big business and will tell you its views: www.cbi.org.uk

THE DOWNSIDE

Some businesses worry that it means that economic policy cannot be tailored to meet the needs of the country. Interest rates have to be the same throughout the group in order to keep the value of the euro stable everywhere. As interest rates are the main method of influencing the economy, it may be difficult to adjust the national economy. This makes controlling inflation and unemployment difficult.

A business which trades mainly with other parts of the world will not be affected as the euro will fluctuate against other currencies just as the French franc or German mark used to do.

Work it out

1 How is a business that you know affected by exchange rates? Draw a flow diagram showing where its inputs come from and where its output goes. Annotate your diagram to show the effects of changing exchange rates.

2 How would being a member of the euro affect the business?

Want to find out more?

How interest rates work?
   See **Going up?** page 54.

The European Union?
   See **Europe together** page 84.

Testing times: AQA

The following questions are adapted from AQA tests.

Assessment evidence	
E6	Identify methods of government intervention and describe how this intervention affects business
C3	Explain why businesses seek to influence market conditions
C4	Analyse reasons why governments intervene to manage the economy
A3	Evaluate the effects of government policy on businesses and the responses of business to changes in policy

What's happened to the jobs?
page 56

1

From the data Longbridge is expected to be competing with a rival plant in Hungary to build a new generation of family cars. The choice will be based on a number of factors, in particular, the amount of aid given to BMW by the UK government.

Source: adapted from BBC News website, 10 March 1999
Courtesy of BBC News Online http://news.bbc.co.uk

a Identify and describe one way in which the UK government could provide aid to BMW. **3 marks**

Assessment evidence: **E6**

Help! Activities that aim to reduce the cost of production can be used to attract or keep businesses in areas that will suffer if business moves out.

Answer

The government can provide financial support in the form of a grant to persuade BMW to invest in Longbridge. By putting up some of the money, it reduces the cost to BMW of investing in the plant.

At the speed of light? page 20
More competitive? page 22

b Describe how UK government aid might affect BMW's investment decision. **3 marks**

Assessment evidence: **E6**

Help! The answer to this question involves productivity and competitiveness, and draws on the ideas of investment appraisal from the finance unit.

Answer

BMW might be persuaded by aid from the UK government because it would reduce the cost of investment. When they carry out an investment appraisal, they would find that, with assistance from the government, the returns on their investment would be better. It would help their cars to be more competitive because they would benefit from new technology, which tends to produce better quality and more production flexibility. It would also increase productivity, so cars could be made more efficiently.

HOW BUSINESS IS AFFECTED BY GOVERNMENT POLICY

c **Examine one reason why the UK government would want to give aid to BMW.** **5 marks**

Assessment evidence: C4

 This question looks at the government's motives. Keeping unemployment low is often high on a government's agenda.

What's happened to the jobs?
page 56

Answer

The government would want to help BMW in order to prevent unemployment. Unemployment is a waste of resources because people who could work are not doing so. There are all sorts of social costs if people are unemployed for a long time. It also has financial implications for the government because more people are eligible for benefits. The revenue from taxation falls as fewer people are working and they are spending less. Businesses earn less and their tax bills are reduced. The government has to raise more money from taxation to pay the benefits. Demand falls, so businesses often go under, creating more unemployment.

It would also assist in supporting the region where the car plant is based.

The government might have a strategic interest in keeping UK-based car manufacturing going.

2   From the data   **Car price law in force**

British car buyers could see the price of new vehicles fall by £1000 or more, as a new law comes into force. The law is designed to increase competition in the industry. Car manufacturers will now have to offer dealers the same discounts as fleet buyers.

The move follows an investigation by the Competition Commission, which showed that British buyers were paying on average 12% more than other Europeans for their cars. The new legislation should bring prices in the UK in line with those on the Continent.

Companies such as Mercedes, Mitsubishi, BMW and Land Rover have already reduced the recommended retail prices for their cars. Mercedes announced just over a week ago that it will cut prices by up to 20% and match UK list prices with those on mainland Europe. However, the two market leaders, Ford and Vauxhall, have yet to move.

The UK government wants car makers to cut the price of cars by at least another 6%. It has given them six months to prove they are offering real discounts to consumers. If they fail to do so, they will face unlimited fines.

Source: adapted from BBC News website, 10 March 1999
Courtesy of BBC News Online http://news.bbc.co.uk

a   **Explain one possible reason why Ford and Vauxhall did not alter their prices at the same time as the other car manufacturers.**

5 marks

Assessment evidence: C3/C4

More competitive? page 22

Under control? page 44

Taking power page 24

Help!   This question asks you to consider material from Section 1 as well as Section 2.

Answer

The uncertainty of the situation may have persuaded these two companies to wait and see what others would decide to do. In a competitive market, the actions of one business often affects the actions of others. By watching the market, Ford and Vauxhall can set their prices at the most beneficial level.

As major suppliers of cars, they are market leaders in the field. They will be less vulnerable to losing market share than other, smaller companies. This means that they can wait and see what happens.

b   Evaluate Mercedes' strategy of immediately reducing
its prices.   **5 marks**

Assessment evidence: A3

More competitive? page 22
Under control? page 44

Help!   This question asks you to think about Mercedes' objectives in cutting prices.

Answer

Mercedes might have wanted to create a good impression with both customers and government. As a top-of-the-market car producer, it might be keen to attract customers from other producers by having a price advantage for a while. The company might believe that once it had persuaded a customer to buy a Mercedes it would be difficult to buy a more run-of-the-mill car in future.

c   Discuss one possible effect of the UK government's car
pricing policy on employment in the car industry.   **5 marks**

Assessment evidence: A3

What's happened to the jobs?
page 56

Help!   This question asks you to think about the effect that the price of the product has on demand, and the subsequent effect on employment in the industry that makes the product.

Answer

By reducing the price of cars in the UK, the government is hoping to increase demand. If demand increases, companies will produce more cars, so more people will be employed.

The price reduction, however, will be on all cars, not just ones made in the UK, so it will affect employment in other countries as well as the UK.

In order to cut prices, the car companies will have to look at ways of increasing productivity if profit margins are to be maintained. There may therefore be longer term gains to the efficiency of the business.

Testing times: Edexcel

The following questions are adapted from Edexcel tests.

Assessment evidence	
E6	Identify methods of government intervention and describe how this intervention affects business
C4	Analyse reasons why governments intervene to manage the economy
A3	Evaluate the effects of government policy on businesses and the responses of business to changes in policy

1 **The diagram shows a typical trade cycle and the problems that occur in the boom and recession periods.**

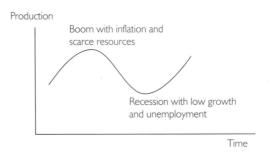

a **Explain why the problems of either inflation and scarce resources in a boom period or low growth and unemployment in a recession period occur.**   **4 marks**

Assessment evidence: C4

Help! This question asks you to explain the theory behind the business cycle.

Going up? page 54
What's happened to the jobs?
page 56

Answer

Inflation is a sustained rise in prices over a period of time. It occurs because people want to buy more than is available. Demand and supply analysis shows how this happens. Prices rise when demand exceeds supply. When resources, like people and machines are in short supply, it is difficult to make more in order to increase supply, so prices will tend to continue to rise.

Recession is a period when the rate of growth slows and may become negative. Stocks build up, so businesses do not want to produce as much. If demand for their products is low, they may lay people off, so unemployment starts to rise. If unemployment rises, people have less to spend, so the downward spiral continues.

b The Bank of England currently uses interest rate policy to remove the problems of inflation and scarce resources in the boom period. Explain how the use of interest rates to reduce inflation would affect the housing market. **5 marks**

Assessment evidence: E6

Borrow - at a price? page 60

 Help! Think carefully about who is involved in the housing market and how they would be affected.

Answer

Most people who buy houses have to borrow money, usually in the form of a mortgage from a bank or building society. All borrowers are affected by changes in the rate of interest. A rise means that the loan becomes more expensive, so people's money does not go as far. Potential house buyers may be deterred because their repayments will have risen, so the demand for houses will fall. As the supply of houses is fairly inflexible, prices will tend to fall.

2 In 1999, the Bank of England raised interest rates on several occasions. The justification given was that this would help to avoid a possible return to inflation. A rise in interest rates, however, has effects on business, and especially businesses in the foreign holiday industry.

a Explain the link between higher interest rates and the rate of inflation **2 marks**

Assessment evidence: E6

Help! This question asks you to make the connection between interest rates, costs and inflation.

Going up? page 54

Answer

Higher interest rates stop people borrowing or increases the cost of existing borrowing. It might also encourage them to save rather than spend. Whichever effect it has, it reduces the amount they have to spend, so demand falls and eventually the rate of inflation will fall.

It also increases the cost of business borrowing, so creates tensions. It may be difficult for a company to raise prices.

b Explain how a rise in the rate of interest might affect Holiweb, which sells holidays on the internet, and suggest ways in which they might respond to it.

Assessment evidence: A3

Going up? page 54
Borrow - at a price? page 60
Changing money page 62

Help! A spider diagram will help you here. Draw a leg for each effect and sub-legs for each response.

Answer

There are three possible effects:

If Holiweb has borrowed money, increased interest rates will push up its costs.

Customers will have less to spend because higher interest rates make borrowing more expensive. As holidays are luxury items, they may be one of the first things to be cut.

If interest rates are high in the UK, investors will want to buy pounds so the value of the pound will rise. This will make foreign holidays cheaper.

Holiweb has some alternatives. It might:

- Try to pass on the increased costs but customers have less to spend so this might not work

- Cut costs to keep prices down. This will depend on the current efficiency of the business

- Improve its marketing in order to attract more customers. It would need to be careful here because marketing can be expensive and there is a trade off between this expenditure and the possibility of potential new customers.

3

> **From the data** The rail privatisation of the early 1990s has created one company which is responsible for the infrastructure of the railways, Railtrack, and a number of train operating companies (TOCs) which are responsible for providing transport services on the railways. The stated intention of the privatisation was to make the railways more competitive, but there was also an objective to move people from road to rail and thereby reduce pollution.
>
> To ensure that the privatisation was successful, the government agreed to subsidise the train operators for the first few years.

a   **What is meant by a 'government subsidy'?**   **2 marks**

Assessment evidence: E6

Government business?
page 50

 Help!   A straightforward question asking for recall. The passage gives you a clue.

Answer

An amount of money given to a company to help pay its costs. The aim is to keep prices down so people will buy more or to encourage the business to produce more.

b   **How might a subsidy affect how Railtrack operates?**   **4 marks**

Assessment evidence: E6

Government business?
page 50

Help!   Think about the effect that extra revenue would have on the business. Remember that Railtrack is responsible for the railway's infrastructure. Its customers are the companies which run the trains and the customers who use the stations. It is not responsible for train fares.

Railtrack might use the extra income in a variety of ways. It could set prices at a lower level in order to encourage the railway companies to run more trains. It might improve the services on its stations to attract more customers to the railways. If it used the money to invest in better infrastructure – rails, signalling etc. – the service would improve, more trains could run and its revenue would increase. If it just wanted to appeal to the short-term interests of shareholders, it might pay higher dividends.

c **Discuss the possible reasons why the government decided to subsidise Railtrack.** **4 marks**

Assessment evidence: C4

Help! This question looks at government objectives.

In need of help? page 48

Answer

The government may have given the subsidy because, without it, no business would have wanted to run the system as the profit margin would have been too low. It might also want to increase rail use, by reducing pollution as people shift from road to rail.

d **Recommend how Railtrack should respond if its subsidy was withdrawn.** **6 marks**

Assessment evidence: A3

Help! Removal of the subsidy will lead to high costs for Railtrack. How can they keep them down? Do they need to? You need to select an approach from the possibilities included in the answer and evaluate a strategy for the company.

Government business page 50
More competitive? page 22

Answer

If the subsidy is cut, Railtrack's costs will rise. It therefore has the choice of absorbing the cut in subsidy or passing it on.

Railtrack sells its services to the companies that run the trains. It therefore has a monopoly because it is a single supplier of space on the track, stations etc. It could simply put up prices and therefore pass the cut in subsidy to the companies running trains. These companies would have little option but to pay the price asked as there is no alternative supplier of this service. The rail regulator might object to this.

Railtrack might decide to run its organisation more efficiently in order to cut costs. An audit of efficiency would help it decide on how, and where, cutting costs would help. It has to be careful in doing this because there are safety issues involved and the company's image could be damaged and shareholder value would fall.

It might also reduce planned levels of investment. By cutting investment, savings will be made but again, this may raise issues of safety and the future growth of the company.

Testing times: OCR

The following questions are adapted from OCR tests.

Assessment evidence	
E6	Identify methods of government intervention and describe how this intervention affects business
C4	Analyse reasons why governments intervene to manage the economy
A3	Evaluate the effects of government policy on businesses and the responses of business to changes in policy

The following questions are based on British Motors, a UK car company facing considerable challenges.

1 a State two ways in which the government might help improve the position of British Motors within the UK and European motor vehicle markets. **2 marks**

Assessment evidence: E6

What's happened to the jobs?
page 56

 Help! A straightforward question asking for knowledge on government assistance. Choose ones that you can explain in section b.

Answer

The government gives financial assistance or help in training the workforce to make the business more competitive.

b Assume the government decides to take action to support British Motors. Describe the likely effects upon British Motors of the two actions stated in part (a) above. **8 marks**

Assessment evidence: E6

More competitive? page 22
What's happened to the jobs?
page 56

 Help! Draw a spider diagram to help you think.

Answer

By providing financial assistance, the government will assist British Motors' drive to increase competitiveness. It will help the business to invest in order to become more productive. This may involve re-equipping the plant or looking for ways to improve quality and add value.

By providing training for the workforce the government will help British Motors to be more productive. If staff are trained in modern techniques, they will produce more cars per head each year. Training may be in either production processes or management techniques. Both can make a business more effective.

HOW BUSINESS IS AFFECTED BY GOVERNMENT POLICY

2 The government's management of the economy has not been helpful to British Motors. For example, some people believe that the policy of keeping interest rates relatively high has been harmful to the UK motor industry.

a Identify one other economic policy adopted by the UK government that may have affected British Motors. **2 marks**

From the data	'The government has also kept close control over government spending which has had adverse effects on British Motors.'

Assessment evidence: C4

> **Help!** The data is helpful but you need to be able to explain the link.

Answer

Limiting government spending means that less money is being put into the economy. The money the government spends goes to people and businesses and means that they have more to spend, so a cut means that they have less to spend on cars.

Going up? page 54

b Explain the possible advantages and disadvantages to the UK economy resulting from the government's economic management. **12 marks**

Assessment evidence: A3

> **Help!** This question asks you to weigh up the effectiveness of the government's economic policy.

Answer

The government's main policy to control the economy has been interest rates. The objective is to keep inflation at bay and this has been successful. This means that price rises have slowed down. Lower inflation gives a sense of stability to people and business.

Keeping interest rates high has kept demand low, as people with mortgages or other forms of borrowing have less to spend because repayments are higher. This means that businesses have to work hard to sell their products.

High interest rates also make it hard for businesses to sell abroad, as their costs are higher because they have to pay high levels of interest on their borrowings. High interest rates can lead to the exchange rate for the pound rising. This is because people want to invest their money in the UK in order to earn good rates of interest. If the value of the pound is high, UK goods are expensive for people to buy, so exports might fall.

Keeping tight control on government spending again reduces the amount that people have to spend and keeps inflation under control. It also means that the money available for the provision of health, education and other government services will be limited.

Going up? page 54
What's happened to the jobs? page 56
Changing money page 62

c Evaluate the likely effects of the government's management
of the economy on British Motors.   **11 marks**

Assessment evidence: A3

Help! Now apply those ideas to British Motors.

Answer

High interest rates limit the amount that people have to spend, so
the demand for cars will be lower. This makes it harder to sell
cars in the UK, so British Motors is likely to find that its turnover
is reduced. This means that it is not working to full capacity and
costs per car will rise. Staff may have to be laid off if stocks
build up. Profit margins will fall and profits will be lower.
Shareholders will, therefore, be dissatisfied with their dividends.

If high interest rates push up the value of the pound, British
Motors' cars will be more expensive abroad, so it will be harder to
export. Residents of the UK may also be tempted to buy foreign
cars as they will be cheaper when the value of the pound is high.

Tight government spending also prevents people spending money as
the government is putting less into the pockets of people and
businesses. This will also constrain the demand for cars.

In order to contend with this, British Motors will have to work
hard to be more productive and improve its competitiveness.

3 MoveEasy Ltd is a family-owned estate agent in Canterford in the
SE of England.

a State three ways that decisions made by the government
and/or the Bank of England can affect the housing
market in Canterford.   **3 marks**

Assessment evidence: E6

Help! Spot three different sorts of policy. Think carefully about your choices. You
have to explain them in the next question.

Answer

Interest rates, income tax, policies affecting employment and control
of the business cycle, environmental planning laws.

HOW BUSINESS IS AFFECTED BY GOVERNMENT POLICY

b For each of the three ways, explain how such intervention might affect MoveEasy. **6 marks**

Assessment evidence: E6

Help! Explain the three that you have chosen.

Answer

Interest rates: increases in interest rates raise the price of borrowing, so loans to buy houses become more expensive and the demand for houses falls. A fall in interest rates would have the reverse effect.

An increase in income tax reduces the amount of money people have to spend, so house sales fall. A cut has the reverse effect.

The government's management of the economy can cause employment to fall and rise. If unemployment rises, fewer people can buy houses, and prices will fall. If unemployment falls, demand for houses will rise.

Other factors can affect the market for houses: if there are changes in planning laws in order to protect the environment it will reduce the amount of land available for building, for example.

Testing times: practice questions

In this section, you are asked to think about how and why the government gets involved with the activities of business. There are all sorts of reasons, ranging from the desire to raise revenue so that it can provide services to the drive to protect the environment.

As the questions in the tests ask you to apply the ideas in the specification to a business, you need to practise on a range of businesses so that you can deal with the one that your awarding body chooses. Try to answer the following using a business you know well or one that you can find information about from the web or other sources. If it is a public company, you may find the annual report and accounts useful to see how the state of the economy has affected it. If a question isn't relevant to the business you are working with, try to find one that does work. A web search of a newspaper will probably come up with an answer.

1 How much tax did the business pay?

2 Has it been affected by any changes in the tax system?

3 Has it received any grants or subsidies?

4 Have any changes in the economic climate affected the business? This might include, for example, a shortage of labour or a rise or fall in demand for its products.

5 Has the business used any of the government programmes to assist business? If so, which programmes and what was the effect?

6 Has the exchange rate had any effect on the business? If so, has the business had to make any changes?

7 Have interest rates had any effect on the business? If so, has the business had to make any changes?

8 Has the business any work relating to the public sector? If so, what is it and what conditions does it work under?

9 How does the business deal with potential pollution? This does not only involve smokey chimneys but includes waste, IT, vehicles etc. Why has it chosen to behave as it does?

10 Is it affected by any EU or UK rulings or guidance on the environment?

11 How is the business affected by legislation to protect the consumer?

12 Has the business been affected by any rulings by the Office of Fair Trading or the Competition Commission? If so, how?

How businesses are affected by international competitors

Great big business?

What's it all about?

You need to understand how multinationals, and other businesses operating in international markets, try to be competitive.

'We need plenty of people who don't cost too much.'

Work it out

1 What is Run Faster Trainers Inc. trying to achieve?

2 Why do you think most of its plants are located in the Far East and South America?

3 What problems may arise if customers think that the company is behaving irresponsibly towards its employees?

WHAT IS A MULTINATIONAL?

A **multinational** company has plants in several different countries. The map shows that Ford has production plants in twenty-five countries around the world.

Businesses may do this because they:

■ need to be close to the market;

■ want to achieve low cost production.

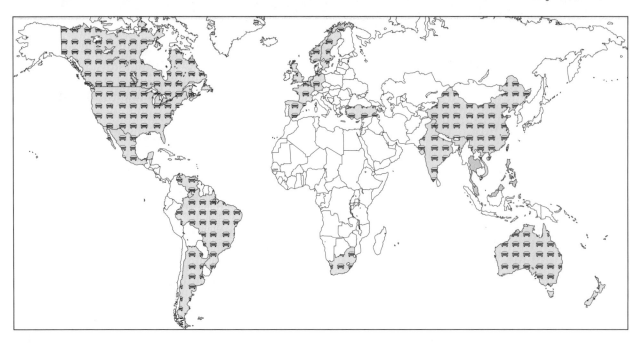

HOW BUSINESSES ARE AFFECTED BY INTERNATIONAL COMPETITORS

Production in most of the developed world is expensive as the cost of land, and particularly labour, is high. By looking for lower cost countries, a company can make its products more competitive.

THE UPSIDE

Countries almost invariably welcome the arrival of a multinational company. It can bring:

- employment;
- extra earning capacity;
- extra spending in local businesses;
- training of staff.

All these factors help the economy to grow.

THE DOWNSIDE

For the host country

Often, profits made by multinational companies are not retained in the countries where their production plants are located. The country does not, therefore, reap the full reward for its contribution to the business.

Some companies have become infamous for exploiting the workforce in their production plants. Many countries have labour laws which are less stringent than those in the USA and Europe. Controls on working hours and conditions raise costs so it is tempting for a business to accept the lower standards in order to produce more cheaply.

Environmental standards are often less restricting as well. Again, costs can be lower if a business does not have to clean up effluent before discharging it into the air, rivers or sea.

Growth is generally beneficial to the economy, but the search for ever cheaper locations means that the company may not be there for long. This creates instability.

For the business

Running a multinational is not always straight-forward. Some countries are very unstable, so it can be hard to plan. Others make it difficult to take profits out of the country. Keeping tabs on parts of the business on the other side of the world can be tricky, especially when faced with different laws and regulations.

This all means that a business needs to set up good communications and have the right expertise to deal with difficult situations. Some might opt to keep investment as low as possible, so less is at risk. The last strategy, however, may not endear a business to its host country as it shows a lack of commitment.

CORPORATE RESPONSIBILITY

Nike and Gap have both received negative publicity for exploiting cheap labour. A poor image can lead to loss of sales and, therefore, many businesses have become much more cautious in the way they deal with staff in developing countries.

Nike have set up a monitoring system which is externally controlled. Information about it can be found on the company website, www.nike.com

BUT REMEMBER ...

No one would support the exploitation of staff in developing countries, but when figures for wages are quoted it is important to consider just what they mean. The cost of living in many parts of the developing world is much lower than in the USA and Europe, so comparisons can be hard to establish. If people were paid the same wages as in the developed world, they would be extremely wealthy. In Vietnam some people who work for Nike are paid better than doctors! This distorts the local economy as the government is unable to pay doctors more.

Work it out

1 Why do multinationals want to produce in the developing world?

2 In what ways may they have:
   (a) a positive impact
   (b) a negative impact on its host country?

3 How does the possibility of bad publicity affect their behaviour?

4 Have a look at the websites of some multinationals to discover their views on corporate responsibility: www.bp.com, www.unilever.com

Trading trends

What's it all about?

You need to be able to explain the effect of the increasing freedom of trade and the World Trade Organisation on the competitiveness of an international business.

'Now the market's global...'

Work it out

1 What opportunities do the igloo builders think might open up in a global market?

2 What issues will they face in trying to sell igloos in a global market?

3 Be creative! Devise a way of selling igloos in warmer climes.

FREER TRADE

International trade provides opportunities for businesses to sell their products to each other. The **World Trade Organisation**'s aim is to assist the growth of international trade. It is an international organisation with a growing number of member countries. Each time it meets, it discusses ways to remove restrictions. It has:

- streamlined the world trading system;

- reduced the tariffs or taxes which businesses pay to export their products;

- protected intellectual property – so people can't steal ideas;

- opened up government purchases to international competition.

Many people gain from trade, although the gains are spread unevenly. If you make T-shirts in the UK, you are likely to lose out because other countries can make them more cheaply. If, however, you are producing a specialist product which requires a lot of expertise, you are probably in a strong position to sell at home and abroad.

A LARGER MARKET

More opportunities   More competition

Many businesses start to sell in international markets when they have saturated the home market. It provides an opportunity to grow. Increased sales can reduce costs per unit as fixed costs are spread further. This makes the business more efficient and therefore able to sell at a more competitive price.

The markets that the business is moving into may be places where incomes are growing strongly or where the products of the developed world are in great demand. Selling in a range of markets reduces risk as economic cycles are not identical around the world.

A bigger market sounds a wonderful opportunity for any business but it must be remembered that it also means more competition. Many countries that are new to a market benefit from cheap inputs which they can sell at a lower price. As trade opens up, more businesses are entering the market so the development of products for a global market requires careful consideration. Social, religious and geographical factors can all affect the desirability of products in different countries.

GLOBAL BRANDS

Look around you. How many **global brands** can you spot. Have you got a can of Coke at hand? Are you working on Microsoft software? So what makes a brand global?

To be global, a product has to be sold all over the world. Sometimes a product has to be adapted a little to meet the needs of a particular country or countries. Being global gives great **economies of scale**. High levels of production and sales reduce costs in most departments, from new product development to production, finance, marketing and distribution.

WORKING TOGETHER

In some countries it is difficult for foreign business to set up independently. In these cases **joint ventures** are often established. By working with a local producer, a business can overcome language and political barriers.

Franchises and **licences** are also used in a similar way. They allow businesses to move into new markets with much lower risk. A franchise allows people to use the product name and trading methods. Selling a licence to a business in another country gives it the right to make the product locally. Beer is often brewed 'under licence' in other countries.

W.T.O. : THE REGULATOR

A country that feels it is hard done by, in trading relations, can file a complaint with the WTO. The USA lost a case brought by India, Malaysia, Pakistan and Thailand. They claimed that the USA discriminated against their 'shrimp' – or prawns as we would call them – because they didn't use turtle excluder devices on their nets. The USA lost because they gave financial assistance to help countries in the Caribbean meet their rules.

Work it out

1   Why might a business want to develop into international markets?

2   What factors should it consider when deciding whether a product can simply be sold as it is or needs adaptation for another market?

3   How can selling in international markets:
(a) increase risk?
(b) reduce risk?

Well protected

What's it all about?

You need to be able to explain the effect that trading blocs, tariffs and quotas have on the competitiveness of international business.

TRADING BLOCS OR TRADING BLOCKS?

A group of countries which gets together to trade is known as a **trading bloc**. In order to reduce competition from outside the bloc, it usually imposes a tax or **tariff** on imported products. This makes imports more expensive.

Despite the work of the World Trade Organisation, the number of trading blocs is increasing. The European Union, for example, is a trading bloc. It has a relatively low external tariff but this can still make a difference to businesses that want to sell into the group.

The North Atlantic Free Trade Area or NAFTA includes countries from Canada to Mexico. Its trade in televisions demonstrates the effect of the bloc. Many US televisions used to be made at home. The creation of NAFTA meant that the country started to buy TVs from Mexico because production is cheaper. Without

NAFTA, the TVs would probably now come from the Far East, where production is cheaper still. Although the USA is now buying lower cost TVs, it's consumers are losing out because of NAFTA.

Trading blocs therefore reduce international competitiveness as businesses outside blocs are at a disadvantage.

Work it out

1 Why is the businessman looking so comfortable?
2 What is the approaching threat?
3 What effect will the removal of tariffs have on business, on the population of a protected area and on businesses outside?
4 Why might the business find it hard to change?

Does business benefit from blocs? The answer is: it depends.

The primary question to be answered is: should the business be in or out of a bloc?

In	Out
A trading bloc provides a protected market so businesses within it do not face such stiff competition. This gives them a much quieter life but can lead to a lack of desire to search for ways to be efficient, so customers suffer because prices will be higher. Protected businesses are in no position to compete beyond their market if they have been taking this leisurely approach.	If a trading bloc has high tariffs, an outside business has to compete hard to sell into it. Being competitive against businesses which don't have to pay the tariff can be a challenge. Sometimes, better service or a more sophisticated product can win the day. Having to work so hard can also improve sales elsewhere because the product is of high quality and competitive in price.

WHAT IS A QUOTA?

A **quota** is a physical limit on the amount of a product that can be imported. They are imposed on particular products and measured over a year. When the quota is used up, no more will be allowed in.

If a country places a quota on video recorders, for example, it wants to protect its home producers. The limit reduces supply and therefore keeps price high within the country, or bloc, which has imposed the quota.

There is a range of other **non-tariff barriers** which countries use to protect their industries. There have been some infamous stories of Japan banning US imports of skiing equipment because Japan has a different kind of snow! Others are more realistic as they are based on health and safety rules. Red tape is also used to make life more difficult for potential imports. Countries also give subsidies to exporters, which, of course, puts them at an international advantage.

All these strategies are against the World Trade Organisation's rules. If they are reported to the WTO, they will be investigated.

Both quotas and tariffs tend to keep prices above the levels of the world market, so customers lose out.

REMOVING RESTRICTIONS

The World Trade Organisation has been responsible for the steady reduction in tariffs and other activities that constrain free trade. As businesses face more competition, the transition can be hard.

Moving from a comfortable state of protection to the highly competitive world market means developing much leaner techniques in both production and management.

Work it out

1 Who benefits from tariffs and quotas?

2 Who loses from tariffs and quotas?

3 What effect does a trading bloc have on the competitiveness of businesses within and outside the bloc?

4 How might a business benefit from the transition process to freer trade?

Europe together

What's it all about?

You need to be able to explain the effect that the European Union, European Monetary Union, and the single market have on the competitiveness of international business.

WHAT IS THE EUROPEAN UNION?

A group of European countries came together to form a free trade area. Since its formation in 1957 numbers have grown steadily. In 2001 there were 15 member countries with a long list of others seeking membership. Over the years, trade barriers between countries have been reduced. No one country can impose tariffs, quotas or other constraints on another country within the EU.

THE SINGLE MARKET

In order to achieve the objective of free trade, it has been necessary to create a level playing field by laying down some rules. If, for example, one country allows child labour, it will be able to make things more cheaply than another country where child labour is banned. A range of other legislation has been passed so that one country does not have an advantage over others.

Work it out

1 If countries are trading freely, why is it important that they all use the same rules?

2 What sort of rules will create a level playing field for businesses?

3 How does a single currency affect business when trading within the group?

4 How does a single currency affect businesses when trading with other countries?

The legislation includes social and environmental controls. Both these factors affect the costs of production, as poor working conditions and a lack of attention to environmental issues reduces costs.

Businesses therefore have to pay attention to these regulations or risk being taken to court. It appears, however, that some countries enforce the regulations more strictly than others.

WHAT'S IMPORTANT FOR BUSINESS?

- An enormous market: there are at least 340 million people in the EU so there are potential economies of scale.

- Trade regulations mean that one model of a product works throughout the market.

- Movement of goods across international borders is more straightforward.

- Investment from multinational companies who want to produce within the EU tariff area.

- Many competitors keeps businesses on their toes as costs must be kept as low as possible and innovation is crucial to keep ahead of the game.

THE SINGLE CURRENCY

The euro was established on 1 January 1999 with eleven member countries. In 2001, Greece joined as well. All countries which have opted in, give up their own currency and use the euro. The currency has the same value in every country. The exchange rate with countries outside the zone is the same wherever you are.

To find more out about the benefits to business have a look at pages 62–63.

The creation of the single currency has led to a move towards harmonisation of economic policy. This has caused anxieties that a country will not be free to control its own economy, because it will be unable to change interest rates to slow inflation or overcome recession.

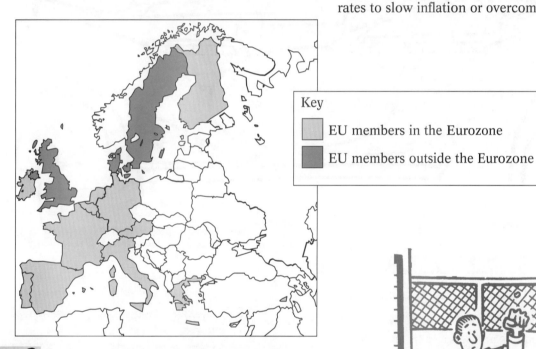

Key

    EU members in the Eurozone

    EU members outside the Eurozone

Work it out

1 What opportunities does the single market open up for businesses?

2 What threats does it pose?

3 Why are businesses keen to be in the euro?

4 What threats may it pose?

5 Use the newspaper and television websites to find out how the euro and the single market have been affecting businesses recently:
www.the-times.co.uk
www.independent.co.uk
www.guardian.co.uk, www.bbc.co.uk

Want to find out more?

Tariffs
    See **Well protected** page 82.

Euro
    See **Changing money** page 62.

An electronic world

What's it all about?

You need to understand how the use of the internet is breaking down international barriers.

'They will be able to do without us soon!'

THE WONDERS OF THE WEB

The internet is changing markets in all sorts of ways. All businesses:

- buy products and services from other businesses;
- sell products and services to customers.

Whichever strategy a business selects, it can cut costs if it gets it right.

The web has helped all sorts of businesses to be more effective. Cheap airlines used to have rows of people answering phones. Now computers do it – almost on their own. Other businesses employ experts in India at much lower cost than experts at home. They provide IT and financial wizardry at a distance.

These are just two examples of how the web has changed the supply chain from business to business to customer.

Work it out

1 How can business to business – B2B – internet communication help a business to be more efficient?

2 How can business to consumer – B2C – internet communication help a business to be more efficient?

3 Why is the business unlikely to be able to do without people?

BUSINESS TO BUSINESS

When buying inputs, businesses are developing strategies to use the web as both buyers and sellers. When Tesco, for example, wants to buy a line it sets up a tendering website for prospective suppliers. This has become known as **e-procurement**.

B2B

➤ e-procurement can save about 10%
➤ Cost of raising an invoice cut by half
➤ Buyers can club together to get bigger discounts
➤ Order tracking is improved
➤ Better management information so stocks can be reduced
➤ Cost of software can be recouped in a year

But, cheapest is not always best. Purchasing departments tend to be price driven and the human element can be lost. Knowing that a company has always delivered, often does not register on the computer system, but an efficient supply chain is crucial to any business.

A bidding process will identify the cheapest, but the outcome must then be reviewed to ensure that the potential suppliers meet wider requirements. Other countries have different laws on labour, social and environmental issues. A company's image can be badly damaged if it is found to be dealing with suppliers that have low standards in these fields.

PLANNING A STRATEGY

To be really effective in either B2B or B2C, a business should take a clean-sheet approach. If it is just bolted on, opportunities will be lost. The power of IT in general is so great that it needs to be built into the whole structure of the organisation.

Sometimes the results may not be instantaneous as customers or suppliers may take time to learn. This needs to be built into costings when decisions are being made.

BUSINESS TO CUSTOMER

Many businesses now have a web presence. Size is no barrier. From the major supermarket chain to the local photographer who wants to show people what she can do, the web can add value and attract customers.

B2C

➤ Saves labour costs
➤ Saves office space and overheads
➤ Automatic invoices save costs
➤ 24-hour working at little extra cost
➤ Customers do searching instead of staff
➤ Easily updated

Some well known businesses have put the web at the heart of their operation. At EasyJet, 85% of flights are booked on the web. The business has rapidly shifted from being telephone-based to web-based. Cost savings are great, as fewer people are needed.

But, a business must be sure that it can deliver. This is straightforward for EasyJet because it just needs to produce a booking that can be printed or emailed. Other businesses have hit problems when their distribution network has been unable to keep up with demand.

For some businesses the internet provides an electronic catalogue. Many still use the paper version as well because customers like to be able to peruse a magazine and make a choice.

Whether the web is just a marketing tool or offers more services to customers, its use should aim to cut costs or increase revenue. If it does neither, the scheme should be reviewed.

Work it out

1 What are the objectives of using the web in business?
2 How can these objectives be achieved?
3 How could the web be used effectively in a business that you know?

Testing times: AQA

The following questions are adapted from AQA tests.

Assessment evidence	
E5	How businesses adapt to international competition and to the conditions found in international markets
E7	Describe the factors affecting international competitiveness in international markets and how businesses operating in international markets are affected by these factors
C5	Show how businesses adapt to international competition and to the conditions found in international markets
A4	An evaluation of the impact of international competition and the effectiveness of their responses to changing conditions in international markets

What's happened to the jobs?
page 56

Who's affected? page 26

At the speed of light? page 20

From the data:	'The Rover Group is considering using cheaper foreign parts for its cars instead of British ones.'

The Group that makes Rover, Land Rover and MG cars says it is examining this decision because the rising value of the pound against other currencies is reducing profits.

This decision could have a serious impact on as many as 200 000 jobs in the UK car parts industry.

Rover buys 85% of its car parts from British companies.

Rover, which is owned by the German company, BMW, could also eventually transfer its production overseas if the increase in the value of the pound continues to hit business.

However, BMW has stressed that it has no immediate plans to switch production abroad and there is no risk to the 40 000 employees at its British plants.

Sources: adapted from the BBC News website, 7 July 1998
Courtesy of BBC News Online http://news.bbc.co.uk |

1   **a**   **Identify and describe one possible effect of foreign competition on workers in the UK car parts industry.**   **3 marks**

Assessment evidence: E5

 A stakeholder question. Remember that it is asking for one effect that you can explain. Don't just list several. It draws on material from Section 1.

Answer

The two main points are:

Unemployment is a strong possibility if Rover starts to buy cheaper parts from overseas. If costs are lower in other countries it will be difficult for UK suppliers to compete and some businesses may shut down or cut back.

A search for increased productivity so the business can reduce costs in order to compete. Employees may come under pressure to increase output in order to cut costs. This may mean working faster or employing new techniques to increase production.
Other possible answers might include: reduced hours, reduced pay or low pay rises. All these would cut costs and make the UK companies more competitive.

HOW BUSINESSES ARE AFFECTED BY INTERNATIONAL COMPETITORS

b **Identify and describe one possible effect that an increase in the value of the pound could have on the price of foreign car parts imported by the Rover group.** **3 marks**

Assessment evidence: E7

Help! Have a look at exchange rates and work out what happens here.

Changing money page 62

Answer

If the value of the pound is high, products from overseas are relatively cheap. Car manufacturers can buy more with each pound if they import than if they buy in the UK.

c **Identify and describe one possible effect that an increase in the value of the pound could have had on Rover's exports.** **3 marks**

Assessment evidence: E7

Help! This is using the same reasoning as the previous question.

Changing money page 62

Answer

If the value of the pound increases, Rover cars become more expensive overseas so exports are likely to fall.

d **An engineering business is thinking about manufacturing car parts for the car industry. Evaluate one drawback of entering the car parts market.** **5 marks**

Assessment evidence: A4

Help! This question meets both Assessment evidence A4 and A1 from the first section of the book. It is important to explain the significance of your answer to get full marks. The question can be tackled in several ways but each one leads back to the fact that a strong pound will send the car manufacturers to look overseas for a better deal.

What will they buy? page 12
Changing money page 62

Answer

Possible drawbacks of entering the car parts market:

Demand may fluctuate because the motor industry, its customer, may look elsewhere for its components. There is already excess capacity in the European car industry so entering a market in which demand is likely to fall would be a foolish move. This provides a very uncertain environment for a business. Most businesses would look for a more stable basis for entering a business as profitability and return on investment would be hard to anticipate.

Fluctuating exchange rates make it difficult to anticipate sales. If the pound is strong, car manufacturers will look elsewhere for suppliers. This provides a very uncertain environment for a business. Most businesses would look for a more stable basis for entering a business as profitability and return on investment would be hard to anticipate.

Testing times: Edexcel

The following questions are adapted from Edexcel tests.

Assessment evidence	
E7	Describe the factors affecting international competitiveness in international markets and how businesses operating in international markets are affected by these factors
C5	Show how businesses adapt to international competition and to the conditions found in international markets
A4	An evaluation of the impact of international competition and the effectiveness of their responses to changing conditions in international markets

1 The United States has recently imposed a tariff on the import of cashmere garments made in Scotland.

a Explain why this might affect the level of sales of Scottish-made cashmere in the United States.   **3 marks**

Assessment evidence: E7

Help! You just have to show that you understand the impact of a tariff.

Answer

Tariffs will increase the price of imported goods if the customers are prepared to pay a higher price. Higher prices will deter some customers, so sales will fall.

Well protected page 82

b Explain why the UK cannot place a tariff on imports from other EU countries.   **2 marks**

Assessment evidence: E7

Help! Trade barriers in the context of the EU. You just need to know that the EU is about free trade among member countries.

Answer

EU rules say that no member country can impose a tariff on another member. The rule means that businesses can compete on a level playing field, so no one is at a disadvantage.

Europe together page 84

2 The euro has been accepted as the new international currency by all EU countries except the UK, Denmark and Sweden.

Analyse how the creation of a single currency area for the euro is likely to affect the competitiveness of UK exporters.   **4 marks**

Assessment evidence: A4

Help! Think about UK companies exporting (a) to Europe (b) to other countries.

Answer

In trade with Europe, the costs of doing business will be higher because money will have to be changed from pounds to euros and vice versa. This means paying the bank a fee. It also depends on the relative value of the pound and the euro. If the pound rises,

Europe together page 84

it will be harder to export because UK output will be more expensive. If the pound falls, exports will be cheaper.

Trade outside Europe will be affected by the relative value of the pound and the euro. If the pound is weak, countries will buy from the UK as their money will go further. If the euro is weak, buyers may source things from Europe rather than the UK.

---

3   **Many firms now choose to set up as multinational businesses.**

a   **What problems do multinational businesses experience in working in different countries?**   **4 marks**

Assessment evidence: E7

 Help!   This question wants you to think about the practical problems of working in other countries.

Answer

Businesses which are based in several countries will face different problems according to their location. Developing countries provide a very different experience from European countries.

Language is an initial problem to overcome. It can take a long time to fully appreciate the culture of another country, so marketing, for example, can be tricky. There may be different laws affecting production, people or the environment, for example. Risk is often higher.

Some countries prevent all profits being sent out of the country or may have higher tax rates if they are. Controlling the business can be difficult when activity is very remote from head office.

Great big business? page 78

---

b   **To what extent could the multinational business overcome these problems?**   **8 marks**

Assessment evidence: A4

Help!   Consider strategies to overcome the problems that you have observed.

Answer

A business might avoid investing large sums in a country that is unstable. Renting offices and factories, for example, removes some of the risk.
It may be possible to keep profit centres at home, so profit is not accrued in other countries.
Local expertise is often the key to success. Many multinationals ensure a strong local representation among the staff. Good communication links are obviously essential to maintain such an organisation.

Success will depend greatly on the ability of the company to be flexible in its approach in different countries. Much of this comes down to management and the role it takes in organising the international aspects of the business.

There is probably not just one answer, as the approach will have to vary according to the market in which the business is involved.

Investing in local businesses is another solution.

Great big business? page 78

HOW BUSINESSES ARE AFFECTED BY INTERNATIONAL COMPETITORS

Testing times: OCR

The following questions are adapted from OCR tests.

Assessment evidence	
E7	Describe the factors affecting international competitiveness in international markets and how businesses operating in international markets are affected by these factors
C5	Show how businesses adapt to international competition and to the conditions found in international markets
A4	An evaluation of the impact of international competition and the effectiveness of their responses to changing conditions in international markets

1 **In the role of management consultant you are to conduct an investigation on behalf of the Board of Directors of British Motors. Either concentrating on sports cars and developing the Swift brand Or merging with another motor car manufacturer.**

Evaluate the two possible proposals and make a recommendation as to which of the two alternatives the company should adopt. 14 marks

From the data	'However, some of the company's brands, most notably its Swift sports cars, have been well received by the motoring media and have generated a lot of good publicity. The Swift range has proved very popular in Europe and sales have increased by 112% over the past five years.'
	'The company needs to raise substantial finance to update production-line technology in all of its factories and to develop new models. Remaining a small independent producer of mass-production cars does not seem to be a viable long-term option.'

Assessment evidence: A4

 Help! You need to weigh up both sides of the argument for each strategy before you come to a conclusion. Some little spider diagrams will help to channel your thoughts. Don't forget to justify your answer. Remember that there isn't one right answer to the question.

Answer

Swift advantages	Swift disadvantages
Good brand name Has customer appeal Small focused production A niche product with fewer competitors Retain independence	Needs investment, which will have to be raised by small company with uncertain future Job losses Few economies of scale

Merger advantages	Merger disadvantages
Become part of larger organisation so expertise can be shared Economies of scale in buying and selling Raising finance for investment easier May retain mass production so fewer jobs lost	Loss of independence Future of company will depend on success in the context of a bigger organisation May lose brand Excess capacity in Europe will lead to further closures so future uncertain Management jobs under threat because of duplication in the two companies

HOW BUSINESSES ARE AFFECTED BY INTERNATIONAL COMPETITORS

Swift could make a successful niche product. It would keep the companies name going and has a chance of long-run success because there is less competition in the sports car end of the market. By increasing efficiency and investing in production, the business could improve productivity.

The merger might be successful because it would take British Motors into a bigger environment which would provide more opportunities for investment and for sharing expertise. New models could be developed with the other organisation, thus providing a more sound basis for the business.

---

2 **Prepare a report evaluating the proposal that MoveEasy Ltd, a local, family owned estate agent, expands its business into France.** **10 marks**

> **From the data:** 'By acting as an agent for British people who want to buy properties in France, we could move into a growing market. We need to consider the impact of the euro on British business and we can capitalise on our prime position in the south-east of England. We can trade freely with European countries and Steve is fluent in French. We have developed fifty years of expertise and have the capital to set it up. We might end up selling British houses to the French.
>
> We have already been approached by a property developer to be sole agent for an exclusive range of villas on the French Riviera.'

More competitive? page 22
Borrow – at a price? page 60
Changing money page 62
Europe together page 84

Assessment evidence: E7, C5

 You need to weigh up both sides of the argument for the strategy before you come to a conclusion. Some little spider diagrams will help to channel your thoughts. Don't forget to justify your answer. Remember that there isn't one right answer to the question.

You could opt for either side but be sure to make a case that holds water.

Answer

France: advantages	France: disadvantages
They have the money to invest	UK not a member of the euro so costs of changing money and uncertainty on pricing
Steve speaks French	Uncertainty about future markets.
Growing market	Buying houses in France is dependent on a range of factors:
Plenty of experience in the UK	value of pound/euro
Personal interest of one member	state of UK economy/state of French economy
of the team	Will need to learn about the legal system and discover how local estate agency
Avoids threats from local competition	works.

The enthusiasm of a team member may get the show on the road. It provides an opportunity to move into a different sort of market. It would, however, be essential to carry out some financial analysis on the proposal and see if the possible fluctuations of the euro make the activity viable.

It would also be necessary to look at some economic forecasts and future trends in interest rates to consider future likely movements in the business, as an approaching recession would reduce demand for second homes.

Testing times: practice questions

For many businesses, the world is now the market. The development of the internet has opened up opportunities for even quite small businesses to sell products and services across the world.

You will need to find a business that is involved in international trade so the local sandwich bar may not prove very helpful! The front of the annual Report and Accounts often discusses the international activities of a business. The World Trade Organisation's website, www.wto.org has a section on trade and business which may give you a feel for the issues.

1 How does international competition affect the business?

2 Has its overseas trade increased in recent years?

3 If so, which countries are most important and has this changed at all?

4 If it has declined, can it explain why?

5 Has it been affected in any other way by trade?

6 What does the business do in order to compete in an international market?

7 Do trade barriers affect the business? How?

8 How does the business view the European Union? Why?

9 Can you think of any counter arguments to the business' view of the EU?

10 Does it consider that joining the euro would be an advantage or a disadvantage? Why?

11 Can you think of any counter arguments to the business' view of the euro?

12 How is the business responding to any changes that have taken place, or might take place in the future?

HOW BUSINESSES ARE AFFECTED BY INTERNATIONAL COMPETITORS

Index

Letts Educational
The Chiswick Centre
414 Chiswick High Road
London W4 5TF
Tel: 020 8996 3333
Fax: 020 8842 7956
www.letts-education.com

First published 2001, Reprinted 2002

Text © Jenny Wales 2001

All our rights reserved. No part of this publication may be reproduced, stored in
a retrieval system, or transmitted, in any form or by any means, electronic,
mechanical, photocopying, recording or otherwise, without prior permission of
Letts Educational.

Editorial, design and production by Hart McLeod, Cambridge
Illustrations by Roger Langridge and Lisa Smith

A CIP record for this book is available from the British Library

ISBN 184085618 1

Printed and bound in the UK

Letts Educational Limited, a division of Granada Learning Limited.
Part of the Granada Media Group.

Every effort has been made to trace copyright holders and to obtain their
permission for the use of copyright material. The author and publisher will
gladly receive information enabling them to rectify any error or omission in
subsequent editions.